EMPLOYEE RELATIONS MIH
HOW TO BUILD STRONG RELATIONSHIPS
WITH YOUR EMPLOYEES

Also available in this series:

making it happen

EMPLOYEE RELATIONS MIH
HOW TO BUILD STRONG RELATIONSHIPS WITH YOUR EMPLOYEES

LAURIE DICKER

ALLEN&UNWIN

First published in 2003 by Allen & Unwin

Allen & Unwin
83 Alexander Street
Crows Nest NSW 2065
Australia

Phone: (61 2) 8425 0100
Fax: (61 2) 9906 2218
Email: info@allenandunwin.com
Web: www.allenandunwin.com

National Library of Australia
Cataloguing-in-Publication entry:

Dicker, Laurie.
  Employee relations: how to build strong relationships with
  your employees.

  ISBN 1 86508 968 0.

  1. Industrial relations. 2 Personnel management.
  I. Title. (Series: Making it happen).

331

Set in 11.5/14 pt Bembo by Midland Typesetters, Maryborough, Victoria
Printed by South Wind Production, Singapore

10 9 8 7 6 5 4 3 2 1

about
the series

making it happen

Are you committed to changing things for the better? Are you searching for ways to make your organisation more effective? Are you trying to help your people and organisation to improve, but are seriously strapped for time and money? If you are, then this Making it Happen book is written specifically for you.

Every book in the series is designed to assist change agents to get things done . . . to make new programs really happen . . . without costing the organisation an arm and a leg and without taking up all of your valuable time.

Each book in the series is written by a top consultant in the field who does not simply theorise about their subject of expertise but who explains specifically how to implement a program that will really work for your unit or organisation. Vital advice on what works and what doesn't work, what tricks to use and traps to avoid, plus suggested strategies for implementation, templates and material to photocopy, and checklists to gauge your readiness—each book in the series is filled with useful information, all written in clear, practical language that enables you to make things happen, fast.

Help your people and work unit to increase their performance and love their work through implementing a program from the Making it Happen series and reap the rewards that successful change agents deserve.

about
the book

The world of work in the 21st century is changing rapidly and it will continue to change at an increasing rate. It is estimated that at least 40 per cent of current jobs, products and services will not exist by 2020. It has also been suggested that the present concept of 'employee' will no longer be appropriate for most people in the future as we move more towards outsourcing work to private contractors or temporary workers. Organisations in the future will be more focused on coordinating external contractors who, in turn, will operate across a number of organisations and industries in a globally competitive environment.

In this changing world of work the traditional master–servant concept of employment will no longer apply. With this comes a shift in focus from traditional industrial relations—with its highly legalistic, centralised, confrontationist approach—to a situation where people management will become the responsibility of those on the spot—the parties involved will deal with each other directly through consultation and joint problem-solving. This requires a shift in emphasis from traditional industrial relations to the more holistic approach of employee relations.

Employee relations are developed within an organisation by all the responsible people. It makes it inappropriate to pass the problems on to a human resources division or to outside authorities. These facilities will still be available as support agencies, but basically you and I now have to take on the responsibility of developing a good working environment for those who operate within and for the organisation. The emphasis under employer relations is more on the recruitment and development of quality people who will gain job satisfaction in a safe, healthy and secure working environment.

Employees will be more confident in the knowledge that they will have equal access to opportunities, be chosen on the basis of merit and will respond more positively to the demands of a changing workplace. Those who survive and prosper in this highly flexible and ambiguous environment will be willing to take responsibility for the development of a positive workplace within their area of operation. People will be encouraged to participate in real decision making in an environment of openness, honesty, trust, cooperation and collaboration. They will have confidence in the knowledge that those in responsible positions have the knowledge, skills and understanding of employment conditions, legislation and regulations to ensure that matters are dealt with quickly, correctly and fairly.

In the past too many people have tended to avoid or only pay lip service to matters such as industrial relations, equal employment opportunity, anti-discrimination, cultural diversity, occupational health and safety and change management. They saw these areas as being the responsibility of someone else or they were matters that were played out in the ring of high-profile tribunals or courts. Those who will survive in the turbulent world of work in the future will recognise that people are our most important asset and their management and development will be their highest priority.

The best operators will be the ones who will manage the creative tensions and differences between employees and be able to blend those differences fairly into effective working teams capable of meeting the challenges of a changing work environment. This will be even more important in a world where employees will work in different environments over a global spectrum linked by advances in technology, with many not even seeing their colleagues or supervisors face to face.

This book is designed to assist you to understand the complexities of your responsibilities in this crucial area of people management and the working environment; in a language and style that is practical, realistic and easy to understand. It breaks down the legalistic jargon into every day applications and it attempts to defuse the threatening image of industrial relations into a more positive approach of employee relations where everyone concerned works cooperatively towards common goals.

about
the author

Laurie Dicker, BA, M.Comm, Dip.T, is a management and training consultant specialising in conducting development programs in the areas of conflict–resolution, negotiation, mediation, change management, leadership, supervision, performance development, team building and career transition. He often works closely in-house with an organisation to design programs specific to their particular needs. He acts as a mediator and is sometimes called in by an organisation to assist with dysfunctional units.

Prior to setting up his own consultancy, Laurie was a Director of Human Resources responsible for HR and risk management for approximately 10 000 staff, as well as training and development, crisis management and industrial relations. He was also a member of a task force that implemented a major change management program in an organisation of 60 000 employees.

Laurie can be contacted through his e-mail: <dicker@smartchat.net.au>

contents

Chapter 4 • Building a better workplace • 73

Chapter 5 • Activities • 97

chapter 1

Developments in employee relations

- The importance of employee relations

- The difference employee relations makes

- Conflict and ways to handle it

- Power, influence and authority

- Change—the new frontier

In my callow early days in the workforce I was asked by senior management to compile the annual statistical returns for everyone in the organisation. This involved gathering statistics on gender, religion, year of birth, etc. for all employees. In an attempt to please my superiors I worked for many hours researching the records to obtain accurate details.

When I was halfway to completing the task I was approached by a good friend who had much more experience than me. He said, 'Don't burst your insides with that rubbish. Get a copy of last year's figures, alter a few of them and then hand it in. It is a totally useless bit of information that nobody looks at anyhow. It is done every year so the system is served, but nobody has enough guts to tell senior management. The only result of all your work will be that the paper will be filed by some statistical boffin in some dark corner of head office where it will never be seen again. Don't waste your time on that crap. Get out there and guide and help the people around you and then you will be doing something useful.'

Welcome to the world of employee relations. This greater emphasis on people held me in good stead when I became a supervisor and manager.

Some employees can work in extreme situations; however, most will require special environmental conditions to operate satisfactorily. Temperature controls, levels of comfort and protection from sickness and injury are essential. They also require periodic time release from operations each day, week and year to recharge their energy cells—unlike diesel motors, they cannot operate continuously and re-fuelling takes much longer and is generally more expensive.

Some people are built like steel and can work under severe physical conditions. Others have the lightness, strength and flexibility of titanium and Kevlar and can withstand different pressures in a changing environment. Others have the gloss of gold and the sparkle of diamonds with values of a different nature. Unlike physical resources, employees talk, argue, demand, question, dispute, think and reason. They are likely to take time out or cease to operate if conditions are not to their liking. They prefer to set their own conditions and will constantly be demanding improvements.

Employees are not machines or gadgets. They are not tasks, functions, processes or products. They are real live creatures that require personal consideration and emotional support, much as they do at home. Also, no two employees are exactly the same. It is extremely difficult to draw up an inventory of employees and impossible to arrange them systematically in warehouses. Any attempt to do so will cause a serious negative reaction and a breakdown in their operations. People are different. When we recognise and value those differences we are well on the way to achieving positive and productive employee relations.

Workers are linked by social, emotional, political and psychological energy bonds. It is important for us, as supervisors, to regularly monitor and manage these crucial aspects of the people who report to us. While people can operate independently, there are certain hidden linkages with others that must be maintained for productivity to continue. An interruption to any one person in a unit, on occasions, can cause a breakdown between the others. On the other hand, it is important to realise that the emotional energies in some people are diametrically opposed to those of others, and any attempt to put those units together will cause sparks, fires and extensive damage. It is therefore important to put people management at the top of your supervisory priority list.

> *A general manager told me recently that he had put a stop to all office emails. He then left his office door open and encouraged people to come in to discuss any issues. That simple action created an obvious lift in morale throughout the staff. They felt they could have direct input into the thinking and development of the organisation and that their ideas were recognised and valued. When issues arose they obtained instant advice instead of waiting in a state of frustration for an impersonal email.*
>
> *In my own organisation I rarely used the out tray for internal mail. Each day I carried my correspondence to the staff and discussed its relative importance. By this approach I was giving advice and guidance face to face while at the same time listening to their ideas and feedback. I also got early warning of any potential difficulties and could therefore set up preventative action rather than wait until disasters occurred.*

Managing the creative tensions between the vastly differing energy bonds of all the employees in the organisation is the most difficult but most important role of supervisors, managers and directors. The management of tasks, processes and products are easy by comparison. Supervisors and managers have to get the people management right because, without it, the other responsibilities don't happen.

If people in an organisation are the most difficult to manage and are so costly in real terms, some might ask why we do not replace them with machines? The answer is very simple. People are the most valuable asset of any organisation and, as many have found to their peril, exaggerated redundancy of staff or the mismanagement of people leads to certain disaster.

■ WHY IS ALL OF THIS IMPORTANT?

Interpersonal relationships and communication within a workplace need to be high on the priority list of all supervisors and managers. It is important to develop a climate of association and a duty of care between management and employees and between the workers themselves. Because workplaces vary considerably, I suggest you look at the following list of simple people management principles to determine which are the most and least important to you and the people with whom you work. Eliminate any you consider irrelevant to your organisation. If you give the list to others in your organisation—both managers and workers—and ask them to do the same exercise you can then compare and discuss the relative differences between your priorities and those of the other people in the organisation.

In detail that means:

- People are the most important asset and have the highest priority in any organisation.
- Everyone in the organisation has a responsibility to create and maintain a safe and healthy working environment.
- People are different and have different needs and concerns and their interests change and are not always clear.
- Conflict and change are inevitable. Change creates an environment for conflict.
- Most conflict occurs because people are different, not necessarily because they are wrong.
- People have a right of association and representation and the right to have equal access to emerging opportunities.
- Merit is the highest priority for selection.
- There is equal access to dispute and grievance resolution.
- There is a healthy negotiated balance between the requirements of the organisation and the demands of the employees.
- People are mostly motivated by self-interest and operate best when they have some ownership of the solution.
- People appreciate honest feedback and prefer to be advised rather than told.
- Most people try to avoid difficult situations and in disputes have doubts about the possible outcomes. They instinctively take positions to reduce their uncertainty.
- People appreciate recognition.
- Management has the right to make decisions for the good of the organisation while workers have the right to have their point of view considered.

All of these principles relate to the good management of people. I have found the most effective organisations give their highest priority to the guidance and support of their employees.

When we start work as youths we are given relatively simple tasks and processes to complete. In these early stages it is our role to complete as many of the tasks to a set standard within a given time period. Over time, we become more experienced and develop more skills, to the stage where it is considered we are able to take on more responsibility.

Initially this extra responsibility probably involves more tasks or more complex functions. Eventually though, it requires the supervision of others within the organisation. For most supervisors, this initially means the writing of guidelines and the overseeing of tasks, functions, policies, procedures, products and customer service. At first these duties tend to be more mechanical with an emphasis on work flow and customer service. But as most supervisors progress further up they find it difficult to let go of these functions because that was what they did best and that was what led to their promotion in the first place. Clearly it is their comfort zone and the focus of their job satisfaction and recognition.

Many supervisors feel they have to continue to show their superiority in task completion to justify their higher status and salary. Their emphasis is always on output not outcomes; efficiency not effectiveness; bottom lines not total picture and cost cutting not balanced budgets. When things go wrong for these people they tend to blame the staff and justify their actions under a cloud of incomprehensible statistical data to prove that it is others who have not met their performance targets. Tasks and outputs are easier to measure and justify than such human issues as health, safety and satisfaction.

In my younger days I looked up in awe at the enormity of the responsibilities of the senior management. Following his promotion to a very senior position I asked a director how he kept control of all his additional responsibilities in an organisation of 60 000. He told me that no one person could fully understand all aspects of the organisation and that the more responsibility one took on the more it was necessary to develop the people around you. You then had to have the confidence to delegate those responsibilities to others. He said that he now saw his role as a guide to the people in his team and a manager of the delegation of job duties. 'My job is to manage the people and their job is to manage the tasks.'

In order to take a more holistic approach, you need to see your role more as a guide, mentor and developer of the people within your area of responsibility. This does not lessen the need to ensure output, efficiency and the quality of the product and customer service within your unit. But it does mean you come at it from a different direction. It means your priority will be the coordination and development of the people who will carry out those tasks and functions. It requires you to develop a safe and healthy working environment in which each person involved can achieve his or her potential.

In such an environment it is more likely you will be able to anticipate most problems before they occur so you can take the necessary steps to deal with them in the early stages, before they develop into major conflicts. It will shift your emphasis from the more mechanical aspects of the job to one where you are involved much more in such things as communication, coordination, problem solving and team building. Look to Activity 1 in Chapter 5 to assess your preparedness to take on these responsibilities.

I always made certain that, at least once a day, I walked around the staff to get a feeling for how things were progressing. I realised people were more comfortable talking to me from their own comfort zone and, until I had shown that I was willing to step out to them, they were not so inclined to come to me in my office. This was not a spying exercise. It was one of feeling the pulse of the workplace. It meant I could become more sensitive to and anticipate potential problems before they arose or developed. It allowed me to also give recognition, reward and understanding to the staff on a regular basis. The staff jokingly referred to my actions as boundary riding and took great delight in telling me there were no holes in the fence.

The degree to which you can effectively coordinate and develop the people in the organisation is a clear measure of your higher skills of management. Who are the real shakers and movers in your organisation? Who are the ones that others follow? To whom would you and others go for advice, guidance and support? Who are the people in control of their own situations and who play a positive role in the development of others? These people are the higher order leaders in your organisation, and it is important for a supervisor to understand the characteristics they possess that give them the respect and recognition in the eyes of others. How might you benefit from following their example?

Supervisors need to look and see; listen and hear; think and understand. In other words, walk the walk; talk the talk. Interacting directly like this does not mean that you have to like your employees or be close friends. It does mean, however, that you will interact with them to the point of having empathy and emotional understanding of their circumstances and how they are progressing at work.

Those who stand rigidly in the distance and shout the loudest rarely see or hear the train coming.

■ HOW IS EMPLOYEE RELATIONS DIFFERENT?

TRADITIONAL INDUSTRIAL RELATIONS

'Wadda we wan? Wenna we wan it? Now!'

'If you don't like it here, there's the door. Get out.'

'I'm the union organiser and I'm calling a stop-work meeting now.'

'You have no right to come on these premises. Joe, call security and remove them from the site.'

'Okay brothers, all out, this is a strike. The management is being unreasonable, unconscionable, coercive and is acting in an arbitrary and unfair manner in contradiction to the award agreement.'

'As from today this organisation is a non-union site and all employees will be required to sign the new enterprise agreement before they can commence work here. If they don't like it here they can leave. Pick up their cheques at the door. They will be replaced by others who are willing to work under our conditions. There is no shortage of people out there who want to work.'

'The union will be lodging a complaint with the court.'

In its purest form, industrial relations could be defined as the means by which people interact in the workplace to determine their outcomes and the conditions under which they operate. Why is it that most people fear or avoid involvement in industrial relations? Because the traditional image of industrial relations is clouded with images of threats, conflict, disputes, injunctions, demonstrations, boycotts, sanctions, damage, strikes, lockouts, pickets, blackbans and other forms of confrontation, all of which have negative connotations that push most people into avoidance rather than involvement. This is not an area for the faint hearted.

During my postgraduate studies in industrial relations the professor walked into the group one evening and listened intently to our deliberations. After an hour he raged into a torrent of criticism and abuse, swearing loudly at each of us who dared to question his ideas or put up an alternative point of view. Having had much practice in the real world of industrial relations he was not afraid to punch holes in our carefully prepared presentations. He questioned and criticised our values, opinions, knowledge and experience. He destroyed our arguments and research and tried to convince us that we had not even a hint of a shibboleth to support our presentations.

When a number of people complained bitterly about his behaviour and language he sat back in the chair, smiled, and quietly told them the facts of industrial life. If they could not handle that level of confrontation in the comfort of a lecture theatre, they should get out of industrial relations and leave it to people who could. Two weeks later the group had reduced by half and consisted of those genuinely interested in the field.

Once, traditional industrial relations was a highly charged arena with macho mountain goats head butting each other into submission. A collective agreement was reached through the dominance of one power over another or through sheer exhaustion. Sometimes a final decision or resolution was agreed on to satisfy the constituents on both sides, even if that solution was to continue to debate or argue a number of unresolved issues. In most cases it was a little like playing football where you only brought in the referee as a last resort.

Traditional industrial relations was managed by select senior members of the central executive of the organisation. They dealt almost exclusively with the hierarchy of the unions. When they could not agree or when one side or the other wished to continue the dispute for political or other reasons, the matter was negotiated or arbitrated by an industrial relations commission or a court. In large organisations it meant that disputes were handled away from where the issues occurred, and in many cases they did not even involve those people on the shopfloor who were involved in the original dispute.

Very few workers, supervisors, managers or directors were directly involved in industrial relations. They left it to the 'experts'. The workers left it to the unions and the others left it to the industrial relations manager or an advocate. The few who questioned authority, wanted to have a say in the organisation of the workplace, or demanded standards of health and safety, were pushed aside or relegated to unfavourable tasks or areas. This was the environment that led most people in the workplace to avoid becoming involved.

I am explaining this traditional approach to industrial relations because many senior managers and union representatives still operate in this manner or believe it is the best way to settle disputes. You need to understand their behaviour in order to look for better ways of developing a more positive approach to human interaction in the workplace.

Industrial relations' prime focus is the resolution of disputes. Ten per cent of people want to resolve disputes by fighting the other side. The other 90 per cent want to avoid it. Neither of these two options is the way to go in modern organisations. This sort of environment led most people to avoid industrial relations and retreat to the safety and secure comfort of managing tasks and processes. It also led many owners and senior managers to avoid contact with unions and their representatives because, in their minds, any such contact spelt trouble. To concede that the unions or workers might have a valid argument meant a loss of face and power that might reflect negatively on their future prospects.

To what extent do you and your organisation follow the traditional approach to industrial relations? Is your approach:

- based on the negative aspects of conflict?
- reactive to problems?
- post–operative in that it happens after the problem has arisen?
- too centralised and remote from where the issues arose?
- primitive and confrontationist in its approach?
- legalistic and therefore adversarial?
- hierarchical and divisive?

- focused on blame, shame and guilt?
- destructive and punitive?

THE NEED FOR CHANGE

To understand the current employment environment we need first to look at how it developed over the past one hundred years. The industrial relations systems arose mostly from the conditions prevailing in the late 19th and early 20th centuries. In those days the proportion of labour to capital was very high and the general levels of skill very low by comparison to today. Labour was the dominant cost of production. Serious depressions and unemployment during that period led to the creation of formal industrial relations systems. These became enshrined in constitutions and legal frameworks and guaranteed that governments had the right to intervene to resolve industrial disputes.

From the early part of the 20th century the shift to secondary industries led to mass production with a work organisation dominated by specialisation, division of labour and large volume production. This was epitomised by assembly lines in car and other manufacturing industries. Individual labour was cheap but, in total, was the dominant cost to industry—a fact that was used to advantage by unions in their bargaining. Workers tended to specialise and the majority stayed in the one industry for life.

With full employment during the 1960s, wages increased and workers believed that life was good, wages were good and the future looked rosy. But that period carried the seeds of its downfall. The scarcity of available labour gave unions enormous power at the bargaining table. Excessive demands for better wages and conditions greatly increased the costs of production.

From the mid 1970s the industrial climate began to change. The barriers to international competition were being lowered, forcing many industries to restructure, downsize or go out of business. It became the period of slash and burn—downsizing, outplacement, budget cuts, mergers and takeovers. The good old days were over; many workers started to question the value of unions and membership began to fall. With unemployment high, workplaces closing down and employees forced into different work arrangements, the comfort zones of the 1960s had disappeared. This process of downsizing and restructuring is still happening regularly and it would be rare for someone not to be affected by it.

The period of protection that led to complacency and inefficiencies was the environment that nurtured the traditional industrial relations systems. It then became confrontationist because global competition was limited. Protection also limited the extent of research, development and innovation. Industrial relations practices gained many benefits for workers and credit must be given to the union movement for substantial improvements in working conditions. But these came at a cost that, in the full light of open international competition, could not stand up.

We are now in a period of uncertainty and ambiguity where change is happening at an accelerating rate. Governments are encouraging privatisation, free trade and international competition, labour is moving across international barriers and there is fierce competition for scarce resources. We are seeing a rapid shift from industrial to information modes of production, and subsequent struggles for power over modes of information and communication.

Labour in proportion to capital is declining as a cost of production. There is a trend in organisations towards restructuring, downsizing and budget cutting, and many functions are now being outsourced. Organisations are becoming more flexible, adaptable and mobile and there is a shift from permanent employment to short-term, temporary, part-time and contractual arrangements. There is greater emphasis on workers pursuing life-long learning, multi-skilling and broad banding, and they are expected to be more flexible and to perform a broader range of functions. Workplace hierarchies have flattened and now have smaller cores of middle- and senior-management, and there is a shift to project management rather than line management. Change is the one guaranteed factor in all workplaces.

> *Workplace opportunities are diminishing within each workplace but are increasing across the global spectrum. A former national, high-profile steel producer was taken over by foreign interests. Soon after, one of the major steel mills was closed and relocated overseas where labour costs were cheaper.*
>
> *A tele-marketing organisation employed three hundred people in this country. Last year they brought in a number of people from India and taught them about the language, culture, politics, social mores and sport of this country. They then returned to India where they took over the day-to-day operations of the tele-marketing work. The former employees were dismissed. So now if you phone this company you might think you are talking to someone locally, but you are in fact talking to someone in New Delhi.*

Old-style industrial relations is no longer appropriate in this changing environment. Some organisations saw the trend early and adapted. Others still continue to use traditional industrial relations practices. Many people in management resist the need for change because they fear that giving in to change is a sign of weakness. They find comfort in dealing with past practices as they feel it gives them the greatest advantage or the least comparative disadvantage. Many have made no attempt to learn or assess other ways— and they will lose in the long-term.

HUMAN RESOURCES

Since the 1970s there has been a shift in emphasis from industrial relations to human resource management, a process that gives greater recognition to the importance of people in an organisation. This period promoted legislation for anti-discrimination and equal employment opportunities. There has been a shift away from the concept of seniority towards selection of candidates on merit, and decentralisation of authority, cooperation, collaboration and team work. Supervisors and managers often joke about this change: 'All my life I have been told what to do. Now I am a manager I have to listen to everyone else.'

Various organisations and industries went about the change process in different ways. There were those that totally resisted change because, to them, a change was an admittance of fault, something that was not allowed to enter their thinking. Many others took a budget or financial approach—when costs exceed price, cut the costs. They adopted a slash-and-burn mentality with staff cuts, outsourcing, redundancies, sell offs, mergers, downsizing and a flattening of the organisational hierarchy. But these managers often lost sight of the importance of people to the culture and effectiveness of the organisation. Many also lost sight of the wealth of corporate knowledge, skills and experience that went out the door when the cuts were made.

The more enterprising organisations realised that there was no one ideal model for change. No one fad or fashion, such as total quality management (TQM) or long weeks spent bonding in the bush, necessarily produced the desired magic solutions. They might have been happy short-term experiences but they seldom produced long-term gains in real effectiveness. The best operators I have seen realised that people had to be the focus of any changes and they took employees into their confidence when planning for and implementing restructuring.

It is hard to generalise, but public companies with an emphasis on satisfying shareholders tended to take more of the slash-and-burn approach. Private companies tended to have a longer-term view and reinvested their returns into the development of the organisation. With the need to rein in the excessive expenditures of the past, governments also tended to lean more towards a pattern of sell offs, outsourcing, privatisation and budget cuts. These were explained as necessary to pay off excessive debts and to remove the government from the job of running a business.

In general, the trend of progressive organisations and their managers, with the focus on the importance of their people, has been towards enterprise bargaining, greater devolution of responsibility and the encouragement of worker participation in decision making. There was a movement away from the rigid in-line, inflexible routines into a cooperative mobile-team approach. This required a change from the domineering, coercive and directive style of management to one based on collaboration and cooperation.

I have found that the best managers clearly identify these aspects as priorities, publicly announce their commitment towards them, set up reasonable timelines for the changes to take place, allocate a budget for the changes and provide the necessary support, training and development to ensure that it happens. Instead of trying to eliminate unions from their work sites they shift the emphasis towards a localised cooperation at the work site. The emphasis becomes one of trying to establish a working environment that is not only safe and healthy but one in which conflict is least likely to occur and where resolution of grievances takes place quickly at the place the problem occurs.

With economic and social development, changes in markets, advances in technology and the greater flexibility of ownership of organisations, comes the need now to dramatically change the approach to dealing with people management. The shift in emphasis towards human resource management was a step in the right direction, but there were still limitations on its effectiveness. In many organisations it was nothing more than an exercise of mechanical personnel management with budget as the bottom line. Many employees did not like being called a resource as they saw it as being equated to machines or equipment.

EMPLOYEE RELATIONS

The 21st century is a time where traditional values are being questioned and changed. We are seeing a demand for open inquiry and a greater acceptance that employees can question and dissent, and there is a strong movement for participation in decision making. There is also a greater acceptance that being different is not wrong, in fact, it can be an advantage. Rather than trying always to preserve the status quo people now see change, innovation and flexibility as beneficial and essential for future success. Also, importantly, there is greater emphasis on quality of life rather than obsession of ownership of property and finances.

There is less emphasis on the strength and power of hierarchical organisations and unquestioned loyalty to them. On average people change jobs every three to four years. In the past this would have been seen as inefficient or disloyal. Today it is seen as progress towards skill and knowledge acquisition. Cooperation, collaboration and inter-dependence are seen as having greater value than rugged, competitive, individualism. In flattened organisations personal and professional growth and job satisfaction are becoming more important than financial security and promotion.

There are many changes happening in the workforce and it is difficult for the average worker or manager to keep abreast of it all. It is also difficult to assess the true value of the various fads that will come your way. Also it is not easy to understand and implement changes in industrial and related legislation when most of us are not legal experts. I have great sympathy for people in responsible positions in the workforce because there are increasing demands on their time and skills; they are expected to do more with less; they are expected to take responsibility at their level of operation and there are fewer support people in management. They are the change agents in the organisation. Constant demands for budget and staff cuts exaggerate these problems.

Employee relations in the 21st century establishes the human factor as the highest priority in any organisation. It emphasises the search for, development of, and continuity of talent and merit. People are encouraged to participate and contribute in a cooperative, collaborative team environment where status and power symbols are minimised. The frenetic urge of the managerial lemmings to throw themselves and others over the cliff has been replaced by a process of consolidation based on merit, talent, emotional intelligence, learning and continuous development. Office barriers are breaking down. Loyalty is earned rather than demanded. People remain loyal to the organisation for as long as it contributes to their development and satisfaction. See Activity 11 on training and development in Chapter 5.

What then are the characteristics of an effective employee relations approach, as distinct from an industrial relations or human resource approach? What is required to deal with modern industry in a time of rapid change? The following is a means of shifting your managerial emphasis towards an employee approach.

The key to your success as an employee relations or people manager is the degree to which you can shift the emphasis of your team from working harder and longer with fewer resources to working smarter with what they have got. The best way to achieve this is to sit down and analyse the potential of each member of your staff. If you assume that 50–70 per cent of their potential has not yet been utilised, ask yourself how you might tap into that pool of talent. Even opening up 10 per cent of that potential will make a considerable difference to the outcomes. If you aim to tap into their intellect, their thinking and reasoning power, their initiative and creativity, staff will be encouraged and feel they are contributing to the development of their workplace, and as a result, their job satisfaction and effectiveness is multiplied. Your key role then is to manage that intellectual input rather than supervise work routines. See Activity 2 in Chapter 5 to assess your readiness to meet this challenge.

■ HOW DO I HANDLE CONFLICT?

Industrial relations came to dominance in the workplace because of the need to deal with conflict, mostly between workers and management. Employee relations by contrast deals with the development of a working environment where conflict is less likely to occur and, when it does, is dealt with quickly and effectively by the people involved.

The workplace, like any other area of life, is made up of people who are different, and conflict in the workplace is a natural result of those differences. Most conflict occurs because people are different, not necessarily because they are wrong. To learn more about this, read another book in this series, *Making Conflict Resolution Happen: A simple guide to dealing with conflict at work.*

A great number of problems and conflicts you will face as a supervisor/manager is caused by people who are considered by others as 'difficult'. They question authority, they won't always follow instructions, they make mistakes, they argue, they make 'unreasonable' demands and they do not always fit into the standard patterns of work, routines, procedures and policies. They require different types of support and guidance. They have different levels of skills and experiences. They even come from different cultures, are different genders, respond differently to humour, have different interests and pastimes and

PRIORITIES AS A PEOPLE MANAGER

Focus on developing attitudes, values and practices that are positive and developmental rather than reactive. Develop a preventative approach to dealing with issues. Encourage your staff to anticipate issues and possible problems and to participate in the decision making of the design and operation of the workplace.

Be confident in devolving responsibility and provide the necessary support to ensure its success. Encourage collaboration, cooperation, group work and cohesion and ensure there is active consultation with greater feedback and recognition. Promote the concept of joint problem solving on site and deal quickly with issues as they arise, involving only those who are party to the matter. Establish a climate of openness, trust and honesty.

Commit yourself and your budget to a progressive training and development program, research and planning. Focus on continuous learning, regularly review, redesign and rotate jobs to prevent boredom, burnout and to enhance development. Actively develop teams that have specific functions but will reform as circumstances change. Clearly communicate your attitudes, values and good practice and publicly commit yourself to their implementation. Allocate resources to ensure these things happen. Shift your approach from master–servant to a collegiate approach in the workplace.

operate at work in different styles. My goodness, does that sound like you and me—the differences between us?

In fact, you and I are both difficult because we are different. Hasn't anyone told you in the past how difficult you can be? I want you to recognise that progress in your organisation will occur only when each person's potential is utilised and the creative tensions that emerge from the differences in the people are massaged into a cooperative team approach. In that environment each person can make a positive contribution, and difficult people like you and me are not pushed into some backwater where it is hoped we will either shut up or go away.

It is easy to adopt a holier-than-thou attitude towards others who appear to be difficult and make mistakes. In fact there are many people who take great delight in finding fault in others. It gives them a good feeling—that they are better or superior to others. They feel that by knocking someone else down it makes them look better by comparison. But this is a very negative approach and does nothing to enhance the quality of the workplace. Think about the people who take that approach in your area of work. How many of those people spend time helping others and building teamwork? How many will accept that the differences between people can be positive? How many accept that change is inevitable? Will they then contribute to and take responsibility for those changes?

Your workplace is not a static or predictable structure. It is not mechanical, even though there are many who would like it to be so. It is made up of people who have different values and opinions, are motivated by different stimuli, are driven by different urges and desires, move in different directions for different reasons and will compete with each other for access to or control over scarce resources. That competition has the potential for conflict. Most of us see conflict only in negative terms but competition is necessary if your organisation is to develop. Without competition and change it will fade away into oblivion.

If we accept that competition and change are necessary and inevitable then we must accept that conflict is also inevitable. Most managers and supervisors will tell you they spend most of their time dealing with the problems created by the few—addressing their arguments, their 'unreasonable' requests and demands. Many find it difficult dealing with union representatives as they see this function as negative, time consuming and stressful. They tend to avoid this as they try to avoid conflict in their lives. Instead of avoidance, address these matters as a regular aspect of your daily responsibilities. It is the manner by which you handle the differences that determine the degree of your success and that of your organisation's.

As a person of influence in your organisation you need to recognise and appreciate individual differences. Evaluate each person's potential and how that might be developed. Look to what each person has contributed and could contribute further if given the necessary support and guidance. Look to the benefits that will accrue to that person, to you, to the team and to the organisation if their potential is developed, their differences are recognised and the creative tensions channelled into positive outcomes. Commence by using Activity 3 in Chapter 5 to evaluate your effectiveness before using a similar model to evaluate those who report to you.

> **As a person of influence in the organisation, see yourself as being in the people business first, and see your prime responsibility as the effective coordination and development of those who work with and report to you. Everything else is secondary to that priority.**

IMPROVE COMMUNICATION

Conflict is a dysfunction of communication. Whenever I have been asked to mediate in a conflict situation or to assist an organisation having difficulties I have found a major underlying cause is faulty communication. Other reasons might emerge at different times but communication will always be a factor. When communications break down there is no way an organisation can operate effectively.

Information is power. You will have to decide the degree that information will or should be shared. If you give too much information people get cognitive overload and switch off. If they are all sitting around committee tables sharing and discussing, who is out there doing all the work? Too little information will result in mistakes and short-comings. Incorrect information is even more serious. It is crucial to your organisation to get the balance and flow of communication right and to constantly test its understanding.

Too many people use their access to information as a source of power. They will withhold or selectively release information according to their desire—to show their status and position or to gain favour from those from whom they will expect paybacks later on. These people restrict the flow of information to you, while they do everything in their power to tap into your expertise and knowledge, and use it to their advantage. They will attempt to disguise this power play in terms such as:

'The information will be released on a "need-to-know" basis.'
'That is the subject of serious discussions at the highest level and I am not in a position at this sensitive stage to discuss it with you.'
'That is not your area of responsibility.'
'Go away. I haven't got time to waste talking. There are more important things to do.'
'Senior management have that well in hand. Don't you worry about it.'

In dealing with major and minor disputes, traditional industrial relations methods had a tendency towards both sides withholding information for as long as possible. 'Keep them in the dark, treat them like mushrooms and feed them compost', was the attitude. The participants saw this as a game of keeping control of the agenda and using it as an advantage over the other side. This still persists in many organisations today. Don't be afraid to ask questions to draw out the relevant information. Questioning is one of the most important strategies in your effective communication kit.

In an open and honest approach to employee relations it is likely both sides in a dispute will put all the information on the table to share. They then collectively test the information, conduct research, and work together towards a resolution through a joint problem-solving approach. Under this model they collaborate, cooperate and pool their resources to produce the most effective outcomes instead of grudgingly giving in bit by bit under sufferance. You should always promote and practice the concept of joint problem solving as a regular workplace strategy. See Activity 12 in Chapter 5.

Take some time out with your staff to evaluate the effectiveness of your communications channel. Ask them to identify what the team does best and what could be improved. Give each group an area to work on and ask them to suggest strategies for development. Rotate the groups so that others can add to the list. Each group will then be given about two to three weeks to research and coordinate these ideas into a plan of action. These are fed back to the whole group for modification, agreement and implementation.

BREAK DOWN TERRITORIAL BOUNDARIES

So many disputes occur because of the real or perceived differences between working units or key personnel in an organisation and the competition for scarce resources, recognition and rewards. The inability of a person or group to perform is often excused by blaming another person or group. Healthy competition in an organisation is a good thing and should be encouraged but only if it produces benefits to the whole and can be kept within manageable limits. It is most effective when people from different units are combined to work on special projects that, in the long run, will benefit all units and employees. Try to break down the barriers between units and encourage people to move between them to broaden their skill and experience levels.

Possessions and territorial 'rights' are often perceived as the basis of security in one's life—in private and at work—and people are often willing to fight to maintain those rights as well as to gain others. Clashes occur when people place different emphasis on those possessions. When one side looks upon a resource as common property, for the benefit of all, they will clash with those who see it as theirs exclusively. Break down these barriers and utilise your coordinating abilities to move the resources to where they are most needed at a particular time and inform all the participants of your reasons for doing so. When you have seasonal fluctuations move your people around to meet these changing demands. Others will accept this more readily when they know that they will receive support in their times of high output.

Look to the indicators of territorial clashes in your organisation.

'It's not fair. Why should we have a budget cut this year when we had the highest output last year?'

'The reason we did not meet the targets was because the finance department did not approve our expenditures on time.'

'That other section gets all the benefits because that is where the boss came from.'

'Young Austin Campbell can get away with murder because he plays golf with the production manager.'

'Our union rules say that you can't do that job. The fitting of metal skirting boards will be carried out by a member of the metal workers union, not the carpenters.'

Territorial competition and demarcations, with their clashes and conflicts are some of the major causes of disputes in the workplace and therefore must be a major focus of attention for your management. Accept the fact that competition can be healthy and productive, and effective employee relations is the art of combining differences in such a way that each person can gain from working with others.

RULES, BLOODY RULES AND REGULATIONS

Organisations do best at what their name suggests, organising. In order to do so they set up patterns of operation that are expressed first in mission statements, and secondly in policies and procedures. These become the structures that produce direction, good order and discipline, so they are necessary if people are to feel secure and safe at work. In your area of responsibility you need to express them in clearly written documents that are accessible to everyone so they become part of an on-going development program.

While 80 per cent of employees complain about rules and regulations they use them as a security blanket and complain most bitterly when they are changed. The other 20 per cent are often thinking and acting towards the future, but too often they forget about the immediate implications of their suggested reforms. This will produce a cauldron of potential conflict and industrial dispute. This is particularly so when people walk across established lines of demarcation and delegated authority.

For those who want and demand change, the rules and regulations act as a brake or governor. But creative people will still tinker with the motor driving the change in order to get more power or speed, or they will travel over more dangerous territory in search of new horizons. The others who sit back and watch have mixed feelings of admiration, awe, fear, jealously and anger. It is like watching the Paris to Dakar world car rally on TV—you're not there but you can see it. This mix is a source of much conflict. The demand for strict adherence to the rules on one side will be a constant irritant to those who implement change and those wanting or demanding change will be a constant threat to those who prefer a stable, secure life.

CATER FOR PERSONAL DIFFERENCES

We are different and act differently in different circumstances. Those differences create the circumstances in which conflict occurs. Those differences are expressed through interpersonal clashes, power plays, arguments, disputes, grievances, accusations, blame, shame, guilt and innocence. They can polarise and, if not well handled, will develop into major industrial or legal wrangles.

Unfortunately, many disputes tend to focus on the people or their characteristics rather than the issue at hand. A respondent to a sexual harassment complaint might say, 'Well, everyone knows she was looking for it. You only have to look at her. She is young, attractive and dresses in sexy outfits. What does she expect? Anyhow, it was all in good fun.' In his defence, a friend might state, 'He is a brain damaged cretin who would have great difficulty finding the zipper on his pants let alone knowing what to do with it if he came across it by accident. He is a harmless fool who wouldn't hurt a fly.' If you were investigating this complaint you need to look beyond the emotions, clear the fog and get to the facts. Clear your mind of pre-conceived attitudes and assumptions and investigate what really happened. See Activity 8/2 in Chapter 5.

Use the same strategies when dealing with people who use personal attacks to gain some ascendancy over others. Compare this type of behaviour with that displayed by politicians. Decide how you will deal with these attacks in the future, whether they are directed at you or at other people.

Separate the people from the issue as a starting point, then gather the facts and deal with them in a logical manner. Recognise and try to defuse the personal issues and differences offered as excuses for unsatisfactory behaviour by looking to the underlying causes rather than the symptoms on the surface. Move in quickly, set the agenda for resolution and get on with the job of resolving the disputes. Recognise your strengths and accept your limitations, but have the confidence to take control of the issues and deal with them. Avoidance is not an option—you cannot walk away from that responsibility or hide in your office behind your emails. Act fairly, honestly, openly and consistently and then others will recognise you as a person who can handle difficulties and resolve problems effectively.

■ DEALING WITH POWER

Power, authority, assertiveness, empowerment and influence make up the fine interconnecting web joining individuals, groups and organisations. They make up the process by which one or a number of persons can modify the actions and behaviour of others. Your group and organisation are made up of individuals, singly or collectively seeking to influence others to think and act in a particular way. It is the interactions between those bonds and the resistances resulting from these influences in your workplace that are the substance of employee relations.

Individuals form a psychological contract with a number of other individuals or groups such as family, work, sport, social groups, community associations, political organisations, neighbours and friends. In each of these groups individuals interact with others by exchanging something for something else. It could be as simple as sharing information during a discussion. In dealing with these interactions you, consciously or subconsciously ask the following questions:

- How much control do I have?
- How much freedom do I wish to have?
- How much am I willing to give up?
- What will I want in return?
- In which areas am I willing to give up my freedom?
- In which areas do I wish to maintain control?
- Which aspects are not negotiable?
- Who am I willing to allow to influence me?

- Whom shall I try to influence?
- What am I willing to tolerate?
- How can I seek out the influences I want?
- How can I stop unwanted influences?
- Who has the power to influence me whether I like it or not?
- Who has the final authority to act?
- Who is paying for it?

In your workplace the use or abuse of these factors are important issues to the development and resolution of conflicts. Monitor yourself and observe others to assess how power, influence, assertiveness, empowerment and authority are used to shape the nature of outcomes. How do you balance your emphasis on each of these factors? How often do you use directive, coercive power? Or are you someone who uses a more subtle form of influence to persuade someone to move in your direction? Do you insist that others recognise and pay respect and deference to your title or position? How assertive are you in getting your message across? Do you encourage and allow for empowerment in others around you? Do you allow them to be involved in real decision making and planning? What real influence have you got in the organisation? Who else in the organisation has a positive influence on others? Who are the movers and shakers that others look up to for guidance and support? They are the ones who best fit the employee relations style of operation.

Employee relations is concerned primarily with the way individuals and groups fit into patterns of behaviour in the structured environment of the workplace. It looks to the manner by which management and employees associate with each other. Power and influence, in one or more of their various disguises, will be the factors in every interaction between individuals or groups and therefore will be the most crucial issues to be addressed by your management. It is about using influence to create an environment of duty of care rather than using power to demand subservience to your authority.

Before the impact of mechanisation, large landholdings were owned by Lords and agricultural work was done by the serfs in what was a true master–servant relationship. Young children were exploited on farms and in mines in extremely unsafe and unhealthy conditions. With the onset of industrialisation workers operated in larger group situations where their combined numbers started to counterbalance the power of owners. They saw the advantages of forming unions, where their collective influence could restore some balance with the financial power of the owners. They started to realise that the withdrawal of their labour was a powerful tool in the bargaining process.

During the 19th and 20th centuries, there were on-going battles between owners and unions of workers in power struggles for control. Over that period workers gained many benefits, though this varied from industry to industry. When there was full employment and a scarcity of available labour the unions were in a more powerful position and made substantial gains. It was a simple matter of demand and supply. When the demand for labour was much higher than supply, the price of labour increased. The 1960s and early 1970s was such a period. In a depression with high unemployment, the unions' bargaining power was lessened, as it did in the 1930s. So the relative power of one side over the other is very much determined by economic circumstances.

Employee relations breaks away from the 'them and us' mentality where constant bickering is the order of the day to one where each individual and group is valued for their contributions and their potential for further development. It recognises that each and every person has attributes, skills and experiences of value to the organisation. These represent power that can be utilised positively for the benefit of all or, alternatively, rejected or restricted in a state of frustration.

You will see that others still use coercive directive power to get what they want. There are many people on both sides of the industrial barriers that still use threats and other bully tactics to gain ascendancy over others. Others use the authority of their position and the delegated power to make decisions. Those with charisma have a personal influence over those that don't. Some people have control over resources and have the say in their distribution. It is this type of power that causes most people to avoid conflicts because of the fear they will be hurt or they will lose valuable possessions or hard-won conditions.

In industrial relations power is often used for the wrong reason. An executive member of an oil company once told me that, on odd occasions, they would create a situation that would result in a strike by the workers. By demanding the workers comply with new unreasonable shift rosters, they knew a strike would result. This gave them the chance to shut down the catalytic converters for maintenance, a process that took about seven days. Because of the strike the company did not have to pay wages during the maintenance period. When the maintenance was complete, the management agreed not to change the rosters or to make minor changes only. Management had the benefit of cost savings for the week and the unions believed they had a victory against the unreasonable demands of management.

When you confront these people use your effective questioning techniques together with your thorough research to get the facts out on the table. In the long run facts will carve through emotions, power displays, tantrums and smoke screens. Knowledge is power. Consciously tap into your powers of logical thinking and reasoning and use that intellect to create order out of chaos. Show empathy, friendliness and compassion to influence others towards your way of thinking. Use your skills and confidence to mediate and negotiate under pressure and establish a credibility recognised by others. You do not have to hold positions of power to do this—you will have power and influence by the very nature of these qualities.

■ COPING WITH CHANGE

The majority of people are stressed by change. Look at the effect upon yourself when relationships in your personal life change; your job changes; you move house; there is a death of someone close to you; you divorce. Look at the anxieties created by the arrival of a new CEO who has announced another restructure of your organisation. Dealing with the known falls into the comfort zone; experimenting with the unknown brings out fears of failure and loss.

Change is inevitable and it is accelerating at an increasing rate. Avoiding it will not make it go away. There is a natural resistance to change that must be addressed if progress is to happen. We used to have a job for life but now, on average, we change our jobs every three to four years. Change is most important to those involved in employee relations—and isn't that all of us supervisors and managers? It is important because the failure to gain a commitment from people to accept change will ensure the change is not successful.

Advances in technology have made a big impact on our private and working lives in the past decade. It is even more frightening to speculate on the future. The size of the micro units that carry information in computers are getting smaller and smaller and it has been estimated that, by the year 2010, these units could be as thin as a few atoms. Richard Feynman, a famous scientist, has predicted that we are fast approaching the stage when, technically, it will be possible to store all human knowledge in a unit the size of a grain of sand. Think about how factors, such as genetic modification and the search for new forms of energy, will change the world during the 21st century and how these will impact on our working life.

Don't panic. Keep your feet on the ground and your focus on the importance of people in the scheme of things. Help build an environment in which they can contribute, play an important role and control their own destiny. That is what employee relations is all about; keep hold of this agenda.

Change is a necessary part of growth. In a highly competitive world an organisation that does not change will stagnate and eventually fade away or drop out of existence. Differences create competition between individuals and groups, which in turn stimulates the desire to experiment with new ideas and approaches. As new challenges appear in a continually changing environment different approaches will be found to overcome them. Changes are often forced upon an organisation by external factors, such as a new government, a new competitor, changes in foreign markets or new legislation.

Change creates the condition for conflict. It results in variations to the working environment and therefore will invite criticism and questioning. There will be arguments over changed roles and responsibilities, appropriate remuneration, health and safety, training and development, costs, redundancies, outsourcing, budget variations, promotional opportunities and competition from outside and location allowances. These are matters that have to be addressed by everyone involved in employee relations.

Look to the signs of resistance to change:

'Let's set up a committee.'
'We have never done that before. Why start now?'
'Why don't you just leave me alone to get on with my job?'
'If it ain't broke, don't fix it.'
'I have been sitting at this desk doing this job well for the past 20 years and
  nobody is going to take that away from me.'
'I'm not trained to do that.'
'The last change didn't work so why should we get excited about this one?'
'Just sit back and do what you have always done because this boss won't last
  long and then we will return to normal.'
'I'm too busy doing important things to spend time on your silly little
  management games.'
'It's not my responsibility.'

If you were the person implementing change how will you address these resistances? The organisation that does not respond will suffer. Our job is to ensure employee relations strategies moves with those changes. As we are dealing with people, this is more difficult but more exciting and more rewarding than dealing with inanimate things. Check your ability to manage change by completing Activity 5 in Chapter 5.

■ CONCLUSION

In this chapter we looked at the factors that are most relevant to the employee relations environment. We have noted the changes that have occurred from the traditional industrial relations focus of the past two centuries to a working environment that gives greater emphasis to joint problem solving in a cooperative, collaborative atmosphere.

The people who work in your organisation and others with whom you have dealings will vary in their approaches to managing people. There will be those who persist with a traditional industrial relations approach. Others who will take a more routine, mechanical approach to personnel management. Some will adopt a developmental human resources style of management. Others, like yourself, will be looking to create a more holistic attitude towards employee relations, accepting that this is an integral part of the role of every supervisor and manager and is not to be left to the 'specialists'.

The language and structures of employee relations

- The participants involved in employee relations

- The processes—negotiation, mediation, conciliation and arbitration

- Awards, agreements and contracts

- The effect of laws on employee relations

In the past, industrial relations tended, for most of us, to be something that was conducted outside our immediate circle. As workers, our involvement in day-to-day discussions about working conditions consisted mostly of complaining about how poor they were. As supervisors and managers we listened to the litany of complaints from workers and sifted through and acted upon the genuine ones. But beyond this immediate environment, the game was played by the big players in the courts and in the media, and we tended to be involved only as cannon fodder for strike action on one side or holding the fort on the other. The average person found it difficult to understand the language, the legal complexities or the processes of industrial relations.

More recently, employee relations made things more localised—decisions were made by individuals or groups and the real issues of people management were addressed at the shopfloor level. The need now is to gain a better understanding of the framework in which these processes take place. The basic dilemma we face is that we all have to take more responsibility for resolving grievances and structuring agreements, for creating and maintaining a safe working environment, and for developing employment contracts without the aid of a legal background and training. We do this knowing that there is still a large and dominant industrial court system to oversee our actions.

Staff are too often forced into signing contracts of employment when they have little expertise in negotiating complex agreements as many organisations resist the interference of unions. This takes away the safeguards for individual workers in the bargaining process because unions have traditionally done the bargaining on an industry basis for all workers. On the other hand, supervisors, managers and those involved in employee relations at the workplace are being forced into the fray with limited knowledge, skills or experience in details of industrial matters. Because of these shortcomings they are fearful of appearing before a tribunal to explain their actions. Many are also so pressured from the top brass to increase production that employee relations issues tend too often to become a secondary issue of management until a crisis situation occurs.

In this chapter I want to lay down a basic foundation of the knowledge and jargon of employee relations because too many supervisors and managers avoid real involvement in face-to-face issues in this crucial area. They become too frightened by the law and its processes. Once you eliminate the fog and mystery of the law you will realise that it all boils down to good common sense and management. It is also important to organise training programs for all of the key people in your organisation as this will give them the necessary confidence to communicate and consult with those around them and prepare them to introduce and develop better strategies and programs to enhance the working environment.

■ WHO IS INVOLVED IN EMPLOYEE RELATIONS?

There are five main players in the industrial or employee arena—the government, trade unions, employers, judiciary and you and me. Traditionally this has been the domain of

employers and **unions** with the **government** in the background as the maker of the rules and as a watchdog on the processes and outcomes. The **judiciary** has had the traditional role of referee and interpreter of the rules. But more significantly now, you and I, as participants in the workplace are now the most important players in the employee relations teams.

> We are all now responsible for creating an environment that will be suitable for everyone in the workplace.

In the past, you and I rarely got to the big game. We mostly watched it on television, read about it in the papers, and talked over coffee about the famous battles that took place. Occasionally, some of us were allowed to carry the sand bucket or sit on the bench, to be called upon only when they wanted to throw some cannon fodder into the fray. But in today's workplace we must take charge of our own destiny and play a bigger role in determining the conditions under which we work.

GOVERNMENT

The federal government still makes laws in respect to conciliation and arbitration for the prevention and settlement of industrial disputes extending beyond the limits of any one

FIGURE 1.1
Employee relations

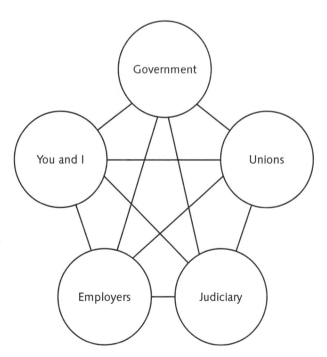

state or territory. It also set up the courts and tribunals to assist with the prevention and settlement of grievances and disputes. The government can also affect organisations and the workplace through other legislation relating to trade, commercial practice, taxation, corporations, external affairs and defence.

At the next level, each state government establishes similar legislation and legal frameworks. This does cause some confusion as to whether any critical matter that comes across your table has to be dealt with under state or national jurisdiction. If uncertain, contact the nearest department of industrial relations and they will assist to clarify your situation. Governments, both at the national and state levels, are also employers in their own right, therefore they can become involved in disputes with their own workforces.

In more recent times governments on both sides have been inclined to encourage the devolution of industrial relations to more of an enterprise and workplace level rather than centralised tribunals. Under this influence courts and tribunals are more focussed on setting minimum standards and acting as a referee as a last resort, although many industries and unions are finding it difficult to come to terms with the new directions and still look to the formal, centralised legal system to arbitrate on their disputes. In general, governments want to retreat from day-to-day disputes because of the damaging political fallout that results from them.

TRADE UNIONS

Trade unions initially grew out of the original craft industries where tradespeople combined into groups to assist each other and to set standards. With the onset of industrialisation, workers combined into industrial unions in an attempt to balance the power and authority of the owners in their push for improved working conditions. The gathering together of large groups of workers in mass production factories provided the environment for the growth of such unions. These have existed for the past 150 years.

With the division of labour and specialisation there was a tendency for unions to be aligned to particular occupations, such as miners, metal workers, transport drivers, electrical trades, etc. These unions represented those trades across the state or country. Later, professional unions or associations in areas such as teaching, health and banking developed. Other unions were created to cover all workers in general areas, such as farming. In more recent times there is a move towards enterprise unions that deal with all workers in one enterprise. These associations have formed to meet the new demands of enterprise bargaining, where the focus is more on meeting the needs of all workers within that organisation or workplace and where the industrial negotiations are concentrated within the enterprise.

When there was compulsory arbitration, state and national unions acted directly or indirectly on behalf of most workers and, in many industries, unionism was compulsory. Unions acted as a watchdog on standards of safety and health in the workplace. They bargained for improvements in working conditions, wages and salaries. Unions opened up communication with management and political powers at the highest levels, protected the rights of workers and provided support in dispute situations. Some people joined unions because of social or political pressure or they did so to gain the security of solidarity of numbers and the association with their colleagues.

In the 1950s, combined membership of unions was greater than 50 per cent of the workforce, with some having close to 100 per cent. Today that has fallen to about 20 per cent. Union membership has fallen because of the decline of manufacturing and other industries in which their membership was traditionally strong, as well as an increase in white-collar industries where union membership was never as strong. The drop has also occurred because of the sharp increase of workers in casual and temporary employment. As we move away from centralised wage fixing to a decentralised enterprise-based system and the increased tendency towards individual contracts, there has been less reliance on the unions in this process.

Despite the decline of union membership you will still need to develop ways by which you can better communicate with them if they exist in your workplace. Look to see how you and the union representatives can work together in a joint problem solving approach to improve effectiveness and productivity and increase the competitiveness of the organisation in exchange for an improved working environment for employees. Most unions today accept that change is inevitable and they try to assist workers in adjusting to those changes. At the same time they try to protect members' jobs and wages by assisting with greater efficiencies and ensuring that workers are provided with the necessary support, guidance and training during periods of change.

It is far better to work with unions towards common developmental goals rather than waiting until crises happen, and then having to clean up the negative aspects of the resulting mess.

Regular meetings with union representatives to discuss issues relating to the working environment and the conditions of employment make it possible to deal with issues before they develop into a crisis. Regular meetings can also provide early warning of potential problems and give you the opportunity to manage the situation proactively. Don't be afraid to work cooperatively with unions, whether they are local representatives or organisers, or those from the central organisation.

EMPLOYERS

National and state industrial systems recognise and encourage employer associations and their registration. These associations collectively represent the employer's interests before tribunals. They see their role as protecting the interests of employers and providing a balance against the power of unions. In recent years they have pushed strongly for enterprise-based bargaining aimed at improvements in productivity and competitiveness. They claim that, unless this happens, further benefits cannot accrue to workers.

Employer associations look for stability in the industrial environment with fewer disruptions to the flow of work through strikes and disputes. They provide advice and support to members and represent employers in negotiations and at tribunals and courts. The larger associations also act centrally to lobby government and change policy. Some of these associations represent members in single industries, such as the Metal Trades Industry Association or the Chamber of Manufacturers, while others cover a range of enterprises, such as the Chamber of Commerce and Industry or the Business Council.

At ground level, individual companies are becoming more directly involved in employee relations and those most likely to survive are the ones that place due emphasis in this area. They are training and employing key people in the employee relations and human resources portfolios. They develop policies and practices that emphasise a cooperative and collaborative approach to change and development, with the employees and employer working together towards common agreed goals.

In this changed industrial environment there is a need to be careful of organisations that refuse to talk to unions, that demand that workers sign individual contracts drawn up by the company, and that use their dominant power of hiring and firing to deny workers their rights. Some of these companies push the boundaries of safe and healthy workplaces in order to reduce costs and they will implement budget cuts, outsource and downsize to increase returns to shareholders with little consideration for the welfare of workers. If you work in such organisations, remember that the industrial relations systems provide minimum protection for workers, and the penalties are high for those organisations that transgress.

TRIBUNALS AND COURTS

Because industrial relations are enshrined in the constitution, they set a legal framework or system that, by its very nature, is adversarial. Therefore, the traditional approach to industrial relations has been one of a battle between competing sides. In too many industries this has been flavoured by a 'take no prisoners' approach.

Various courts and tribunals have been established to adjudicate on matters of industrial law and to act to resolve industrial disputes. In very general terms, courts tend towards acting as a third party to arbitrate or make judgements in industrial disputes. Commissions and other tribunals tend towards acting through conciliation, whereby a third party commissioner tries to assist the disputing parties to come to an agreement. Commissioners are more likely to make strong recommendations in the first place; when they give orders, though, their decisions will be supported by the full force of the law.

If you have to attend a court or tribunal, you will find that it is a formal legal hearing, but it is not so daunting as other courts. In dispute resolution they are more likely to emphasise a negotiation approach, and are less concerned with the rules of evidence required in a normal court of law. Regardless of which side you represent, you must go to the hearings well prepared but expect to be asked to put forward and explain various

STRIKES AND LOCKOUTS

There has always been a traditional struggle for power in the workplace. The employer on one side has the right to hire and fire and controls the wealth and operation of the enterprise. They have the power to make decisions in regard to what will be produced and how it will be done. They have the power to start, stop, continue, expand or contract the operations. They can choose who will be employed, where and under what conditions.

On the other side the workers have their labour, skills, knowledge, understanding and experience. Their greatest power is their ability to offer or withdraw their labour. Individually, this might have little significance on operations, but, collectively, workers have considerable impact. It was for this reason that workers joined together to form unions—so they could balance the economic wealth and power of the employers.

Strike action, or the collective withdrawal of labour, is a very powerful tool in the hands of the workers and is mostly used only as a last resort. A lockout is a powerful weapon that is used as a last resort by the employer. Consider this scenario:

'Chainsaw' Dan had been appointed to drastically restructure Mucluc Constructions. On the day after his appointment he announced that the electrical section was to be outsourced to private contractors. All tradespersons would combine into one group and would be expected to work in any area determined by management. The workforce would be cut by 30 per cent, with a further reduction of 20 per cent after three months. Within seven days every worker would have to sign a new individual work contract drawn up by management. Refusal would result in instant dismissal.

Dan called in the union representative and declared that Mucluc Constructions was now a non-union organisation and that any industrial activity would result in dismissal. Fred, the union representative slowly turned and called to the workers, 'Okay lads; all out; stop all work; turn off the machines; there will be a stop work meeting at the Trades Hall in an hour to consider the harsh, unjust and unreasonable demands of management.'

Dan called out to the operations manager, 'Lock the gates and don't let anyone back in unless they are willing to sign the new employment contract and work under my conditions. Advertise for other staff to replace these rebels.' As he left the property, Fred turned to Dan and said, 'We will see you in court tomorrow.'

The propensity for strikes and lockouts like this is declining rapidly. As people become better at negotiating at the local level strikes and lockouts will become even less of a factor in the workplace.

options to be considered for possible resolution. You will be asked to respond to the proposals of the other side. Prepare yourself by anticipating what the other side will put forward. Do your research and have the facts to support your proposals. The commissioner might call a halt to proceedings to set aside time for you and the other side to give further consideration to the matter, for example:

'Mr Jones, the other side has considered your proposal. They have stated that they will not accept it in its present state but they might consider the first two points if you were willing to accept the last point of their earlier proposal. Would you be willing to give serious consideration to that proposal? We will now break for an hour, after which we will return and listen to your response.'

With the greater emphasis on enterprise negotiations, the involvement of courts and tribunals is declining, despite the fact that they are trying to maintain a central focus and control on industrial relations. Their role today is more concentrated on the determination of minimum wages and conditions, making judgements on the interpretations of awards where they still exist, dealing with unfair dismissal and making judgements on appeals.

To gain a greater knowledge of the industrial relations systems relative to your state, industry, union and organisation contact your nearest department of industrial relations. They will be more than happy to assist in providing information and explanations in a user-friendly manner. These days they have a strong emphasis on educating and supporting the people at the local level. If necessary you can also approach legal experts who specialise in employee relations. Many unions and organisations will use these legal people, or others experienced in industrial relations, when they have to go to court or the commission. There is a strong tendency to use them also for matters involving workers' compensation.

YOU AND ME

Each and every one of us has a responsibility for employee relations whether we are workers, supervisors, managers or owners. In the highly regulated systems of the industrial period, labour was a dominant cost of production and trade unions were a dominant influence on the conditions prevailing at the workforce. Today, mass labour is not as critical to production as it once was. Labour is becoming more focussed on individual knowledge and effort, and is more highly mobile and flexible. The growth of the information society has changed the landscape. More is being produced with less physical input by people. Your competitive advantage now, and in the future, is based more on your knowledge and intellect rather than your physical skills.

As the emphasis on mass labour declines there is less demand for traditional trade unions. There is less emphasis on centralised wage negotiations and determinations—we no longer listen to the news every three months to hear the latest changes to the national wage case. There is now more emphasis on individual negotiations or group agreements at the enterprise level. It is important, therefore, for you and me to become aware of and skilled in this area and to take more responsibility for our own destinies. We will be required most often to negotiate our own contract of labour, which will be more than just a monetary remuneration as it will involve all the conditions under which we operate.

Just as important is our role in ensuring a safe and healthy workplace. In the past, workers tended to leave this to management. Today it is everybody's responsibility. Current occupational health and safety legislation is very clear as to the responsibilities of all of us in the workplace and the penalties for breaches of the conditions. I suggest you contact the local authority for occupational health and safety to get their latest literature. They produce excellent, easy-to-read guides and they will run courses and serve as an adviser. Ignorance can't be used as an excuse in this important area.

> **Working conditions have been the major area of on-going disputes in the workplace and still are.**

■ WHAT ARE THE PROCESSES?

Employee relations concentrates on providing and developing the conditions under which we work and then finding the answers to any problems that arise from them. As we are all different and the conditions under which we work differ, there will be continuous discussions about them. This requires skills and understanding about the basic processes that we use to settle our differences. Although there are many variations of these processes let me explain the four main ones that you will use—negotiation, mediation, conciliation and arbitration.

NEGOTIATION IS A DAILY EVENT

This is the process by which two sides will sit down and talk to each other—raise issues, explore options, consider the differences—and then come to some agreement by adjusting the options to a point where both participants are satisfied with the changes. This is the most common process used by everyone in their day-to-day life and at work when making decisions, putting order into your life or resolving disputes. It can be as complex as deciding the fate of a multibillion-dollar industry, or as simple as deciding on who uses the bathroom first.

> 'If you use the bathroom first I will stay in bed and catch up with the news.'
> 'No. While you use the bathroom I will get the breakfast and then you can drive me to work.'
> 'I will agree to that if you give me a kiss first.'

Agreements don't have to be formal and written into contracts. They do not have to be complicated by intense struggles. Too many of us tend to avoid bargaining or negotiating because of the negative image that has developed in major conflicts and their portrayal in the media. We fear the possibility of losing our valuable possessions or becoming too confused in the hurly burly and intensity of the discussions or arguments to the point of losing control of our own agenda. The end result of negotiation is change and that frightens those who like the comfort of the status quo.

Any attempt to change the nature of the conditions under which we operate or to change another person's behaviour will involve negotiations, unless, of course, you force that change by brute strength. Always consider negotiation as a process of giving up something in order to gain something else, with the end result being agreed to by both parties because they see the end result as being better for both. The two key words in negotiation are **if** and **then**:

If I accede to your unreasonable demands, **then** I expect you to agree to my unacceptable offer.

'**If** you require me to be on standby during the weekend **then** I would expect an increase in my salary.'
'I cannot afford to increase your salary until productivity improves.'
'**Then** I ask to be supplied with a company vehicle.'
'**If** you agree to do standby **then** you can use the vehicle only at the weekend.'
'**If** I agree to that **then** I ask that my salary be reviewed again after three months and be increased **if** productivity improves.'
'Agreed. After the productivity improves in your area we will sit down to discuss variations to your contract.'

Negotiations have great advantages because they involve you and I directly in the process and, because of that involvement, there is a commitment by both of us to the final outcome. There is no third party involved. There is more likely to be a better understanding of the facts and a greater sense of ownership of the process. Both you and I have to take responsibility for the momentum of the proceedings but this does result in the satisfaction of having some control over our own destinies. On the other hand it can be very time consuming, costly and draining if it is allowed to get out of control. There can be an imbalance of power and authority, especially when one of us does not have the necessary skills and experience of negotiations. Limited access to information also restricts the effectiveness of the process.

When you are in negotiations try not to maim, destroy or belittle the other side because negotiations are a long-term process and they build on long-term relationships. Try to build bridges, establish a climate of openness, honesty and trust and provide easy access to information. Do not focus on the difficulties, faults and the past; don't concentrate on the matters that divide you—instead, focus on the common aspects that bring you together. Use the path of cooperation and joint problem-solving, not the rugged hills of competition.

Use Activities 4 and 13 in Chapter 5 to sharpen your negotiation skills. For further information, see another book in this series, *Making Negotiation Happen*.

MEDIATION IS AN ALTERNATIVE TO CONFLICT-RESOLUTION

Mediation involves the use of a third party to assist the process of coming to an agreement. The mediator controls or facilitates the process but does not make decisions or determine the agreements. Their role is to help you and the other party clarify the issues discussed, determine who speaks and for how long, manage the setting and accommodation of the meetings and control the conduct of the discussions. The mediator acts as an independent facilitator who does not take sides but who assists the participants to focus on a joint problem-solving approach.

If you are party to long, drawn-out dispute you might suggest the use of a mediator to assist and speed up the process. On other occasions you might be asked to act as a mediator. At work, this might be difficult as you know the participants and it is hard not to take sides, or appear not to do so.

In its purest form mediation does not allow the mediator to recommend or decide the outcomes or the direction the agreement will take. This has the advantage of ensuring the participants reach agreement between themselves, thus ensuring a commitment from both of them to the outcomes. In practice, the most effective mediators flavour their actions with a touch of conciliation to assist the process, especially if one or both sides are intransigent.

If you are acting as a mediator, look for issues that have the greatest potential for agreement and concentrate the focus on options that appear to have some value. Ask the parties to work through building or modifying those options. In this way the parties are constructing something positive rather than trying to destroy the opposition in order to gain some ascendancy.

'Could I focus your attention on some of the points you have raised? The union representative has just outlined a proposal that appears positive. Could we look at that in conjunction with points 2 and 4 of the management's plan. I think there could be value in developing these further. Could we break for an hour so that each group might consider these developments further? When we come back I want you to determine if there is value in combining and developing these aspects from both sides into a coordinated approach.'

When acting as a mediator I suggest you meet with each party separately to listen to their complaints and to crystallise the critical issues as they see them. Feedback your interpretation to ensure its accuracy. This is a listening and questioning session. Then arrange a meeting place that is non threatening. Clarify to both parties how the meeting will be conducted and how and when each side will take an active part. Assure them they will have an equal opportunity to participate and that your role is to act as an impartial facilitator and not to take sides.

Discourage 'you' statements that are negative, accusatory and demanding of the other person. Ask them to focus on the issues, not the persons involved. Look for and highlight any agreements. Emphasise the positives of a joint problem-solving approach.

I was once on a task force that had the responsibility of implementing significant changes in a very large-scale organisation. This followed an independent review that had put forward 22 proposals for modification. The union had conducted a large public and political campaign of opposition to the changes.

At our first meeting with the heads of the union the chairman of the task force acknowledged the strength of the union's feeling against the proposals but he then asked the head of the union to highlight any proposal with which they agreed. After a short discussion we found that there was general agreement by both sides on 14 of the proposals; cautionary or limited agreement on another five and total opposition by the union to the remaining three proposals. The chairman then asked both sides to focus on how we might jointly implement those proposals with which we all agreed.

Through these simple acts, the tone of the meeting changed from one of potential disaster to one that was reasonably positive and productive.

The advantages to mediation are:

- the mediator is independent
- the parties work together towards agreement
- there is greater commitment to the outcomes
- the process is controlled
- it is less expensive than court proceedings.

The disadvantages are it can be time consuming, it can be difficult if there is an imbalance of power, and it takes time for the parties to get used to the process.

CONCILIATION IS A POWERFUL AND EFFECTIVE STRATEGY

This is the process by which the disputing parties use a third person to assist them towards agreement. It differs from mediation in that the conciliator can make strong recommmendations as to the outcomes. It differs from arbitration in that they don't make final decisions. It is far more informal than court procedures. In the workplace you can use the conciliation process on a day-to-day basis to resolve disputes or solve problems between individuals or groups.

> The conciliator acts as a facilitator rather than a judge and, if they see value in a proposal, will recommend to the other party that they seriously consider it.

When you act as a conciliator you look beyond the immediate fight with its negative connotations and high emotions to the probable resolution and agreement. You rise above the dust storm on the ground, look for the most likely path to progress, then lead the participants towards resolution. You will know when to accelerate, slow down or brake according to the prevailing conditions, and you will use your knowledge and experience to guide the parties to agreement.

In a more formal sense, conciliation is a process used by an industrial commission. They use every attempt to reach agreement with the cooperation and active participation of both sides. Unfortunately, in the past this process involved mostly the hierarchy of management and unions who made decisions away from the workplace. Now, it is more common to involve the people directly concerned in the dispute. If you have to appear before a commission remember that it has the status of a court with all the formal trappings, but the conduct of the proceedings are less intense. The process is aimed towards finding some agreement and acceptable outcomes in an environment where the rights of all participants are more likely to be protected within the terms of the law.

Conciliators come from a variety of backgrounds and are very experienced in employee matters. They are sensitive to the needs of those not experienced in tribunal proceedings. They are not afraid to give advice or break to defuse emotions and relieve tensions. They are equally adept at punching holes through false images and blowing away smokescreens. If you have to appear, then be prepared to openly consider other options put to you or to seriously modify your own proposals. If you do your homework first you will be in a better position to do just that. This process is not a fight to the death; it is one of joint problem solving with a strong and experienced guide to assist the process.

The advantage of conciliation is that there is a third party to assist, but in a less threatening environment than a court. It is less confined by rules of evidence, by the law and by precedent. It attempts to get the parties to talk with each other, rather than against each other. You will feel you are contributing to the outcomes and have the opportunity to put proposals forward for consideration. On the other hand, the strong intervention of a third party making recommendations might result in a lack of commitment from one or both parties to the outcomes. It is set in a quasi-legal atmosphere that can be threatening for some people. There is a disguised or real threat of penalties if you don't comply with the recommendations and, too often, it is seen merely as a pause in the real fight.

ARBITRATION BRINGS QUICK AND DECISIVE RESULTS

This is a process in which the conflicting parties can't agree and the agenda is taken over by a third party who acts like a judge and jury. The third party will listen to the cases and arguments from both sides and make a binding decision that locks in the outcomes for both sides. For the big issues in the employee relations area, arbitration is conducted mostly in an industrial commission or court, or in a number of tribunals such as the Equal Employment Opportunity Tribunal. Matters relating to such things as workers compensation or public administration are more likely to be dealt with in this manner.

While arbitration in its purest form is conducted in a court or tribunal, the process can be used in the day-to-day management of disputes at the workplace. Every day, you, as a supervisor, manager or director, will make arbitrary decisions on a whole range of issues. There is little time under the pressures of work to sit down on every issue and have a meeting of the minds. There is the danger that you could spend most of your time at consultative meetings and little of it actually putting things into practice. Arbitrary decisions, made on the run, permit the work flow to continue until the matter can be addressed at a later meeting. This is quite reasonable providing matters, such as safety, are addressed immediately.

Arbitration is also applied in the workplace where there has been a breach of discipline or when a person appeals against a decision resulting in their dismissal or non-selection for a position. Many managers consider it a waste of time conducting such formal hearings because they believe it is their sole right to make such decisions and they believe that no correspondence should be entered into. Increasingly they are finding out that, should they not observe due process at the workplace in handling these matters, the issues will be taken out of their hands and dealt with by an external court or tribunal. It is far better to learn how to do it properly at the workplace than to lose control of the agenda to someone you have never seen before.

Arbitration is quick, relatively inexpensive and it provides an independent third party to make the decision. Decisions are made and actions taken. Everyone knows the extent of the outcomes and the sanctions that will apply should they not be followed. On the other hand, the decision was not the result of agreement between the participants because it was determined by an independent person. This often results in a lack of commitment to the outcomes by the participants.

Arbitration suffers from the adversarial overtones of the legal process when the emphasis should be on cooperation and joint problem solving. The negative aspects of penalties and sanctions do not assist collaboration and cooperation. Too often the deep-seated problems that led to the dispute are likely to re-emerge in a different context at a later date. The problems are not resolved, merely shifted to get temporary relief.

■ SETTING THE CONDITIONS

Over time there have been a number of changes to the processes that have been used to determine wages, salaries and other conditions at work. The following is a description of the terminology used in these determinations and how the emphasis has changed.

AWARDS

An award is a legal determination that clarifies the minimum pay and working conditions that must apply in a particular industry or occupation, and as such is enforceable by law. The determination of awards has been the traditional means by which the Industrial Relations Commission or courts have determined the conditions of work and the levels of wages and salaries. The award is determined following a dispute from one or both parties—the employer and the employees, or the unions representing them.

Although enterprise bargaining is becoming more prominent, awards still apply in the majority of workplaces and enterprise-bargaining processes use the award as the foundation for changes in working conditions. Awards provide the benchmarks for determining the level where there is no disadvantage in any future determination. Some awards are registered at the federal level while others are restricted to the state, although the emphasis on federal awards is being reduced.

It is important for mangers to understand the terms of the awards covering all employees, to display the conditions in the workplace for all to see and to ensure their implementation. They will need to be referred to on a regular basis to ensure all requirements are met. If there is any ambiguity in their interpretation a meeting with the staff or their union representatives to clarify the issues will need to be called.

A variation to an award occurs after a dispute is lodged with the Industrial Relations Commission or court. This is normally in the form of a log of claims lodged by the employees or the union and rejected by the employer. If both parties agree to the outcomes then it is registered as a consent award. Where there is no agreement it is referred to arbitration for a decision by the commission. In recent years, the content and coverage of awards has been reduced and they apply more as minimum standards or safety nets.

Although the publicity surrounding negotiations will always emphasise wages and salaries, awards do cover many other items such as:

- classifications and required skills
- terms of employment—permanent, temporary, full-time, part-time, casual
- hours of work and their variations—meal breaks and overtime conditions
- minimum wages to be paid to each classification, including industry and equipment allowances; rates for juniors, trainees and apprentices; piece rates and bonuses
- conditions relating to termination of employment, including redundancy payments and stand-down provisions
- leave conditions, including annual, long service, carers, sick, family, bereavement, compassionate, cultural, study and parental—maternity, paternity and adoption—annual leave loading
- public holidays
- penalty rates
- jury service

- superannuation
- grievance procedures
- uniforms, laundry, travel and incidental expenses, and other allowances such as first aid certification.

AWARD RESTRUCTURING

The highly centralised conciliation and arbitration process started to lose its impact from the early 1980s when the costs of labour were increasing while the country was finding it difficult to compete on an international scale. From that time there has been greater emphasis on restructuring industries with the aim of improving efficiency and competitiveness. There was a need for the labour force to be more skilled, flexible, efficient and competitive. At the same time, workers were attempting to share more equally in the fruits of improvements in productivity and to gain more job satisfaction. There was a shift of emphasis away from industry and occupational awards towards enterprise determinations.

Agreements then concentrated on skill-related career paths, multi-skilling and broader ranges of responsibilities for workers. There was a breakdown of the demarcations of the past. Work practices that allowed for more flexibility were encouraged. This process required people to become more conversant with employee relations issues. Supervisors, managers and human resource specialists had to prepare proposals that led to greater efficiency, effectiveness and increased productivity.

For those in positions of responsibility in the forefront of employee relations, it is now necessary to consider wage negotiations in a more holistic manner—wages are only one small part of the package. With promotional opportunities reduced, employees today are more interested in how the workplace can stimulate their intellectual capacity, the extent to which it gives them job satisfaction, how it might extend their skills and knowledge and how their potential is being developed. Wages are merely one aspect of their rewards.

WORKPLACE AGREEMENTS

In certain circumstances employers and employees can agree to set up a workplace agreement that, in simple terms, is a written agreement between them about the terms and conditions of employment. It must be signed by both parties and has to be approved by the official Employment Advocate. Any such agreement must pass the no disadvantage test, which means that the employee must not be worse off than under a previous award.

If you are involved in such an agreement seek advice from your employer organisation or union or the Department of Industrial Relations.

CONTRACTS OF EMPLOYMENT

In general terms a contract of employment is formed when an employee accepts an offer of employment and the conditions under which that employment will take place. In doing so, however, both parties accept that they have certain rights and responsibilities under the law. Even though the contract is not formed under an award or enterprise agreement there are still safety nets and provisions that must be met. Although these might not be specified in the written contract, both parties are obligated under law to meet certain minimum requirements.

Employers are expected to:

- pay wages within 14 days and reimburse employees for work-related expenses
- ensure a duty of care for all employees and create and maintain a safe and healthy workplace
- act in a non-discriminatory manner and provide equal opportunity
- refrain from acting in a manner that could damage the reputation of an employee
- work to build positive relationships with their employees
- be open and honest in their dealings with employees
- meet all their obligations in relation to occupational health and safety, taxation, superannuation and insurance
- ensure that minimum employment requirements, such as leave entitlements, are met.

The employees, in turn, also have obligations that include they:

- obey all reasonable demands of the employer
- take all necessary steps to maintain a safe and healthy workplace and inform the employer of real or potential dangers
- have the necessary skills, training and experience to perform the task or provide the service, or act under due guidance
- exercise due care in the performance of their duties
- account for any monies or equipment received and pass on any invention or initiative of a product or process invented during their employment
- pass on any information relevant to the employer's interest
- be loyal to the employer by not doing anything that might sabotage or lessen their competitive position.

I provide a word of caution here. Be certain to check the fine details of any contract of employment. If necessary have it checked by a lawyer, or seek advice from your relevant union or employer association. Ensure the contract is signed by both parties. Ensure both parties have copies of the contract. Ensure the contract clearly states the roles and responsibilities and the terms of employment. When you are involved in contract negotiations be open, honest, truthful and fair. The commitment that this will generate will more than compensate for any possible gains that could have been achieved by subterfuge.

John Jones applied for an advertised job and was called in for an interview. He was told the general conditions of work, including the hours, meal breaks and the rate of pay per hour. When he accepted the position and turned up to work he was asked to sign a contract. In the small print it specified that John was to be employed as a private contractor or sole trader, totally responsible for his own insurance, superannuation and taxation. Any leave and meal breaks taken were to be at no pay.

John knew that the additional costs substantially reduced his net pay and he was denied the normal legal rights and protection of employees. If he took out private insurance it was at a high cost; if he didn't, he put himself at considerable risk of high expenses in cases of accident and injury. If he took out all the necessary insurance cover and met all the other costs of being a sole trader his take-home salary would have been less than 50 per cent of the package offerred. This was far less than that paid to employees in similar positions elsewhere.

He had been enticed into the position under false pretences and misinformation. When he queried these conditions with the employer and informed him that he had gained legal advice from the union, he was told the job was no longer available and was shown the door.

NEGOTIATING AN ENTERPRISE AGREEMENT

An enterprise agreement is specific to a particular enterprise or project and is negotiated voluntarily by the employer and employees, or the union acting on their behalf. The enterprise process allows for the employment conditions to reflect the needs of the organisation and the input of the employees. The matters negotiated in an agreement are much the same as in the previous awards but are more likely to include other issues. When you are negotiating an enterprise agreement consider it as a whole package. Look to the following as possible inclusions in the agreement:

- changes to the manner by which work is organised
- the nature of the working environment
- the means by which productivity will be improved, including greater flexibility
- the development of a culture of improvement
- improved training and development to meet emerging needs and to enhance productivity
- better coordination between capital and labour
- consultative processes in a conflict–controlled environment
- job redesign and rotation
- career path planning and opportunities for improved job satisfaction
- sharing of the gains
- greater emphasis on customer satisfaction

- best-practice strategies for change management
- on-going monitoring linked to continuous improvement programs.

While a list such as this is positive, there is often a great difference in the vision, ideals and reality of the negotiators. After a hundred years of the traditional industrial relations system it has been hard for established practitioners to change. A cultural change of this significance is not easy to achieve. As a result there are many agreements wrapped in the new trappings of enterprise bargaining that are nothing more than a tweaking of the old awards thrashed out by former champions of the industrial big ring—you can still read about these disputes in the papers almost every day.

All enterprise agreements must comply with state and national law in regard to minimum entitlements. They might cover the employees of one or a number of employers or those involved in a special project. They must be agreed upon by the majority of the workers or by a committee elected by the workers to act on their behalf. A union may act on behalf of the workers. Every agreement must contain procedures for grievance resolution. The initial agreement will replace a specific award and will have a life of one to three years, but will remain in force until replaced by another agreement.

It is advisable to have these agreements registered with the appropriate industrial authority or commission. Agreements must not be signed under duress and employees must have sufficient knowledge, information and understanding of the process. The processes leading to the agreement should be open, fair and appropriate. No one can be forced to sign an agreement. However, when an agreement is reached by a secret ballot of the employees, then every employee is covered by that agreement even though they were not in agreement with the provisions. Any new recruit is also covered by that agreement. All employees and new recruits must have access to the agreement in a language they can understand.

The problem most likely to be faced is if the people on the other side of the table do not understand the process of enterprise bargaining and they might approach it like a property and custody settlement after divorce. Some will still persist in the confrontationist mode of traditional industrial relations. I suggest an expert be brought in beforehand to train people in effective bargaining. Follow this by structuring appropriate procedures for all to follow. See Activity 14 in Chapter 5.

In order to eliminate some of the problems that might occur in your situation, you will need to understand to what extent the members of your team understand the details and purpose of the agreement process. Enterprise agreements are part of a wider agenda of organisational and economic change. Wages, salaries and working conditions should not be treated in isolation. They will be seen best in the context of change and as part of the objective of improved productivity and effectiveness. It will be difficult for you to continue to trade off hard-won working conditions for increased productivity. With successive enterprise agreements there will be very few that can still be used as bargaining tools.

There is increased stress created by any change. The stress created by inexperience in negotiation will impact on the final result, especially if the negotiations become drawn out. There will be added responsibility on everyone. There will be additional pressure on employees to keep up with continuous learning, multi-skilling and broad banding. The constant threat of job cuts, re-locations, downsizing, outsourcing and redundancies adds to the stress levels. There can be a perceived imbalance between the returns that might accrue from improvements in productivity which are passed on to the shareholders against those passed to the workers.

There is often inadequate training and experience of management in employee relations issues. There can be an over emphasis on task, function, process and product rather than people management, resulting in people being treated like physical resources.

You should see enterprise bargaining as an opportunity to introduce positive employee relations policies and practices. You need to start from a holistic strategic approach involving all stakeholders along the way. Instead of sitting back and waiting to be told what to do, you need to be out there making change happen; always ensuring that you take the people with you. You are the one who can lift their minds from the minute detail of tasks to the future directions that will lead to positive changes in the culture of the organisation in which everyone benefits.

■ WHAT LAWS ARE IMPORTANT?

As you and I are now more directly responsible for the development and maintenance of a good working environment, it is important for us to understand the main pieces of legislation that affect the workplace. If you are anything like me you probably find that reading transcripts of the law is about as interesting as watching grass grow, and trying to interpret the legalese is like translating ancient Sumerian hieroglyphics.

If this is the case then go to the government websites or to the nearest department of industrial relations, equal employment opportunity tribunal or occupational, health and safety service to get the relevant information in a user-friendly manner. Put yourself on their regular mailing lists to receive newsletters containing up-to-date information. Many of these publications give examples of case studies that are easy to read and understand, and can be used for discussion at your regular staff meetings. Industrial law also varies from country to country and state to state so you should regularly get updated copies of all of the legislation appropriate to your workplace.

The following is a summary of the relevant acts you should be aware of.

WORKPLACE RELATIONS ACT 1996
This is a national piece of legislation in Australia. It shifted the emphasis from a centralised system of industrial relations to one where the prime responsibility rests directly with the

employers and employees. The influence of formal third parties was also reduced. At the national level the courts and tribunals are now focussed on ensuring minimum standards for all organisations and providing safety nets for all workers. Also highlighted are the importance of freedom of association, the avoidance of discrimination and the need for all enterprises to improve productivity in the face of increased international competition.

The legislation encourages enterprise bargaining through the negotiation of workplace agreements. These can apply on an individual basis, to a special project team or group, or cover all workers in the enterprise. The difficulty for most enterprises is breaking away from the former centralised models and the dependence of third parties to settle disputes. This legislation puts the responsibility where it should be—at the enterprise or workplace where the real work happens.

INDUSTRIAL RELATIONS ACTS

To confuse the issue, each state in Australia also has legislation relating to industrial or workplace relations. These acts have some provisions that cover all enterprises and other provisions that cover organisations that operate under former state awards. They also give particular bias to their individual demands in the areas of occupational health and safety, anti-discrimination, cultural diversity, freedom of association and enterprise bargaining. You will need to obtain your local state guides to ascertain the importance of each provision to your enterprise or workplace. You could also invite experts in these areas to conduct training sessions with key people in your organisation.

ANTI-DISCRIMINATION AND EQUAL EMPLOYMENT OPPORTUNITY ACTS

These two acts apply at both state and national levels. While there might be slight differences in the wording, collectively these pieces of legislation work on the basic premise that:

- people who are treated unfairly or who are denied access to opportunities will not perform at their optimum levels
- poor individual performance will reduce the effectiveness and productivity of an enterprise
- it is illegal to discriminate or harass others
- employers are liable under the law for any discrimination or harassment that takes place at work
- if you are responsible for the supervision or management of people you represent the organisation and therefore you, together with your employer, can be held legally liable for breaches of the Act.

To be on the safe side you will need to be aware of the combined factors of discrimination covered by all state and federal laws. These state that you must not discriminate against or harass employees or recruits on the basis of characteristics such as:

- gender
- pregnancy
- race or ethnic cultural background
- religion
- marital status
- disability
- sexuality/homosexuality
- transgender/ transsexuality
- age
- political beliefs
- union membership
- family and carer responsibilities.

See Activities 6 and 7 in Chapter 5.

To actively remove discrimination from your workplace you need only adopt a low-key manner on a day-to-day basis, such as:

'John. Please remove those nude photos from the wall.'

'Andrew. Could you please look after Mustapha during his settling in period. His English is poor so he will need special help with written procedures and safety signs. Get him in contact with English language classes. We will assist with his fees.'

'Mary. Your crude sexist jokes are not appreciated. Keep them out of this workplace.'

Ensure you support your daily actions with a planned program of training and development in this area.

OCCUPATIONAL HEALTH AND SAFETY ACT

Every employer is required under the Act to accept a duty of care for the health and safety of everyone in their workplace. This duty of care extends to designers, installers, manufacturers, contractors and the self-employed. Supervisors and senior managers are held responsible for breaches of the legislation. It is important therefore to translate the provisions of the Act into practical applications at work. This requires effective communication and training.

The Act emphasises the importance of duty of care, the establishment of health and safety committees, clear policies, consultation, identification and assessment of hazards, risk management, emergency procedures and the improvement of workplace layout and design. It also emphasises the importance of rehabilitation for those injured at work.

You need to ensure that each of these matters is covered in practical policies and procedures in your own organisation. Do you have adequate safety procedures? Are policies and signs written in a language that can be understood by all? Have all the staff been trained in OH&S? Is OH&S a part of every induction program for new employees? See Activity 9 in Chapter 5.

FREEDOM OF ASSOCIATION

Various pieces of legislation ensure that employees or independent contractors and employers are free to join or not to join an industrial, professional or industry organisation. Both national and state laws prevent discrimination by an employer or industrial organisation against someone because they are a member, or not a member of a union or employer association. A person cannot be discriminated against because they:

- are a union official or representative
- have been involved in industrial action
- make a claim for a legal entitlement
- become involved in a political activity that does not interfere with their work
- provide information about an employer who breaks the law.

Legislation also covers those who have right of entry to the workplace and the conditions under which they may do so. Compulsory unionism is now unlawful and workers are protected against coercion or discrimination on these grounds. Although there has been a limited response, there are now provisions to allow for enterprise unions rather than those based on trades, professions or industry.

UNFAIR DISMISSAL

Various Acts allow for an employee, who believes they have been unfairly dismissed or have been threatened with dismissal, to present their case to the Industrial Commission or a court. Too many employers are obsessed with the thought of legal action relating to these provisions and demand the right to dismiss anyone as they see fit. This applies particularly to those in small business. You will often hear employers complain that the law is loaded against them and that it is almost impossible to dismiss an employee. On the other hand employees complain about the unfair and unreasonable actions of employers who dismiss workers without due regard for the law.

In between all of this huffing and puffing the laws do provide clear guidelines relating to the dismissal of workers. It is not as big a problem as most people believe, and most of their fears can be eliminated by the use of common sense and good management practices. Employers can avoid the problems in this area if they follow best practice in the recruitment and employment of people. (In the next chapter I will outline simple guidelines to deal with this important area.) See Activity 8/1 in Chapter 5.

chapter 3

Employee relations in the workplace

- How to deal with grievances

- Recruiting the best person for the job

- How to dismiss staff when things go wrong

- Compensation for injury and illness

Employee relations is a process of managing diversity, flexibility and change, and is the responsibility of everyone—not just those who occupy positions of authority.

It is everyone's responsibility to develop and maintain a working environment that is effective and productive, one in which each person can grow and develop their potential for the good of the enterprise as well as for their own personal and professional satisfaction and rewards. However, the first step to achieving this goal is for you to commit yourself publicly to this ideal and to follow up that commitment with practical implementation so that everyone can see you are serious about these matters.

Diversity, flexibility and change can create the conditions for conflict, so much of the employee relations processes focus on the management of conflict situations. The principle objective, therefore, is to create an environment in which conflict is less likely to occur and, when it does, to have open and honest processes to deal with it for the benefit of the organisation and those who work there.

Since 1990 there has been a shift of emphasis from the highly centralised industrial relations systems to the current localised enterprise bargaining. With this shift, the nature of conflict–resolution has also changed. The number of days lost from strikes has been dramatically reduced but major industrial conflicts still occur in large, private organisations—especially in the building, mining and transportation industries, and in the public sector. There are far fewer strikes in smaller organisations.

On one side of the coin, this could be seen as beneficial to enterprise and the economy because of better work flow and fewer disruptions. On the other side, however, this must be measured against increased resignation rates, job dissatisfaction, staff turnover, low morale, unemployment and fewer opportunities for progression resulting from the constant changes and greater diversity, flexibility and competition. All of these matters impact on an organisation.

It could be argued that the traditional industrial environment was more effective because there were more union organisers and representatives and more senior managers who specialised in those areas. Many of these people worked behind the scenes in areas such as staff welfare, rehabilitation, counselling and legal advice. These matters formed the bulk of day-to-day industrial management and those people worked almost exclusively in conflict management and developed an expertise that was lost when unions became less influential and specialist industrial relations and human resources managers had a reduced impact in a flattened hierarchy. It could also be argued that employee relations is everyone's responsibility and it is more appropriately placed in the workplace where it happens.

You need to assess the current situation in your area of responsibility with regard to employee support and rehabilitation. Is it truly working?

Organisations are now much flatter, resulting in fewer rungs on the traditional promotions ladder. So the challenge to employee relations specialists, and all of those people in positions of authority or influence, is to create a working environment where each person can gain recognition and job satisfaction. Employees should be recognised more for their knowledge, skills and experience and should be given the opportunity to work in a range of areas where they can expand their interests and involvement and be given other rewards for that involvement. The focus should be on their ability to guide and develop others and to encourage others to be more willing and capable to take on responsibility. In the best organisations rewards go to those people who are willing and able to be involved in design and development, are directly involved in decision making, will accept responsibility at their level of operation, can solve problems and can work to develop a cohesive supportive team.

Once you have stated your commitment to improving employee relations you need to take your staff into your confidence and take time out with them to discuss and formulate improvements in this area. This does not require a great injection of funds, just the input of intellect, design and implementation. Consider such matters as skills audits, job redesign, job rotation, delegation of responsibility, relieving in higher positions, flexible hours, job sharing, permanent part-time work, project management, working from home, training and development, recruitment, induction, career-path planning, succession planning, mentoring and consultative committees for a start. Ask for and listen to the staff responses to these proposals. Work as a team to redesign the workplace into an involved committed entity.

In this rapidly changing environment with its uncertainty and ambiguity, conflict, both real and potential, is the dominant factor to be managed. Not only do you have to manage the creative tensions caused by diversity and differences but you will also have to be ahead of, or in control of the pressures and stress of unpredictable change. Central to this good management is how you manage the resolution of grievances.

■ WHEN GRIEVANCES ARISE

The underlying thread that binds the employee relations approach to people management is the positive, proactive development of a working environment in which people are involved in shaping their own destiny in coordination with those around them and those to whom they report. Why then should I be emphasising grievance resolution that appears to be negative and reactive? The reality is, conflict is inevitable, especially in today's rapidly changing environment, and yet too many people in positions of responsibility avoid it at all costs.

In highlighting the need for grievance resolution I want to promote those approaches that will encourage early intervention and joint problem solving. The more you are seen as a person willing and able to move in quickly and effectively in this crucial aspect of people management, and the more open, honest and truthful you are, the more trust and respect this will generate. This will more than compensate for the anxieties you will have in dealing with conflicts, and will encourage people to come to you openly when problems first appear and before they develop into major crises.

Grievances occur when employees become concerned with the manner by which they are being treated by their employer, management or other workers, when employees believe there are faults or deficiencies in the workplace, or when employees believe they are not gaining sufficient recognition or reward for their efforts and contributions. They will also bear a grievance when they believe there has been a breach in their enterprise agreement or contract.

Conflicts are a little like mushrooms: they grow well in compost and will quickly enlarge the more you try to push them away into dark places.

PRINCIPLES AND PRIORITIES

Before looking at the practicalities of grievance procedures let's look at the basic principles underlying the good management of those procedures. Employee relations is based on the principle that employers have the right to manage and regulate their own organisation providing they do so without being unjust, unreasonable, harsh or oppressive to their employees. Ethics, integrity, good behaviour and conduct are often the casualties of the fierce world of competition. Respect will be at its highest in organisations that develop an environment where ethical behaviour is promoted and valued and where standards and conduct are clearly enunciated to all concerned. Each and every person, whether a new recruit or the general manager, has responsibility for their own area of work. It is best when this is clearly stated and understood by all.

Challenging ideas instead of people will encourage the greatest input from participants. People are more positive and productive when their ideas are valued and are part of the discussions. Building bridges, partnerships and relationships through cooperation and collaboration are far more effective than the destructive forces of competition. While a person's rights are important, the needs, concerns and interests of individuals, groups and the organisation have a higher priority and must be taken into consideration. Earning the trust of those around you, rather than demanding it, is the foundation of quality relationships and the key that opens the door to resolution.

Openness and honesty are crucial to integrity and respect, while fairness and acting with good reason are fundamental to good management. You need to promote the concept that joint problem solving is superior to competitive point scoring. Balance the need for free expression with active listening and understanding. Understand that people's expectations will vary and the management of the tensions created by these differences is crucial to resolution. People have the right to support and guidance.

HOW TO PRESENT A CASE

At various times you will be involved in settling disputes or jointly solving problems. This mostly happens at the workplace but you could also be called upon to appear before a court or tribunal. For the inexperienced this might seem frightening but it boils down to the basics of preparing a reasoned, logical, sequential presentation that is, as much as possible, based on facts and in a manner that can be easily understood by all present. No one is perfect, but the most effective negotiators have a high proportion of the characteristics in the checklist on page 54.

Don't have a panic attack if you do not meet all of the requirements in the checklist all of the time. It is extremely rare to find anyone who meets the ideals of this model under all circumstances. Let's face it, we are human and we are dealing with other human beings. Take confidence in those qualities that you do possess and try to identify those that you can best work on to improve your abilities as a negotiator.

In dispute situations you could be acting on behalf of yourself, the employees, the union, the employer or the organisation in general. As such you will be an advocate for that particular cause. Your greatest advantage is that you will know the workplace and the people in it and therefore can speak from the facts instead of clouding issues in legal jargon. The people around you will appreciate straight talking and facts instead of gobbly gook and legalese. See Activity 8/4 on Chapter 5.

Facts will always beat fog and emotion.

The heads of industrial tribunals and courts appreciate advocates who are well prepared and can communicate their case in a logical manner based on facts. They are more impressed if you can show you have been implementing best practice in the workplace. If you have not been doing so, identify the shortcomings and then suggest strategies for overcoming them. They also appreciate it more if you are willing to consider a range of options when trying to reach agreement rather than coming to the table with a stubborn attitude and a locked mind. Remember, negotiation and conciliation are processes of exchanging values—'**if** you are willing to do this **then** I am prepared to accept that.'

If you prepare a list of the advantages and disadvantages of each option in advance then you will have greater control over the agenda and will be more able to focus other people's attention towards your priorities. If you know what you are willing to trade in order to achieve something and know what is not negotiable, then it is easier to maintain the momentum towards resolution. If you go in unprepared you will be limited to responding to other people's proposals and fighting rearguard actions rather than being out front constructing bridges towards a joint resolution.

EFFECTIVE NEGOTIATOR'S CHECKLIST

Assess your skills by ticking those that are your particular strengths. Circle those that you consider you could respond to better with further development.

Ability to plan, prepare, research and analyse a situation ☐

Ability to develop a range of options for resolution ☐

The understanding that negotiation is the exchange of one value for another ☐

Ability to gain access to information ☐

Effective communication skills ☐

Ability to recognise personal and organisational interests and needs ☐

An understanding of the environment and those who work in it ☐

Ability to test options and assumptions against the facts ☐

Ability to direct the energy of a meeting towards common ground and agreement ☐

Ability to think clearly under pressure ☐

Willingness to take risks ☐

Acceptance that change and conflict are inevitable and that they can be positive and productive ☐

Willingness to make decisions ☐

Objectivity ☐

Integrity, openness, honesty and trust ☐

Persuasiveness, persistence, determination and patience ☐

Calmness and self-control under duress ☐

Power of logical reasoning ☐

Ability to remain focussed in the midst of distractions ☐

Ability to generate respect and rapport with people on all sides of the table ☐

Following his dismissal Scott Andrews went to the Industrial Relations Commission claiming he had been unfairly treated then dismissed, and that the manager, Simon Smith, had been harsh and unreasonable in his treatment of him. After much questioning and discussion, Commissioner Campbell asked Scott what outcomes he wished to achieve. Scott replied that he wanted his job back. The Commissioner asked Simon if he was willing to take him back. Simon had anticipated, in the spirit of conciliation, that other options would have to be considered.

He first made it clear that Scott could not be placed in his former position because he had been responsible for a number of accidents and, despite training and support, his continuing employment in that area, or any other field position, jeopardised safety for himself and others. Simon then offered to employ Scott in a clerical position under his direct supervision for a probationary period of three months. If that were successful he would be made permanent in that or a similar position.

Commissioner Campbell turned to Scott. 'Mr Smith has made you a reasonable offer that I believe you should seriously consider. If you wish to take up his offer you should contact him before this time next week. We will meet here again at 10 a.m. next Friday to finalise this matter.' Scott used the next week to find employment elsewhere as he did not like the thought of working in a clerical position under the direct supervision of the manager.

The important matter here was that the manager was prepared to look at alternatives and put them on the table without sacrificing safety.

WHY GRIEVANCE PROCEDURES FAIL

If you are aware of the reasons why grievance procedures fail you will be better prepared to avoid them in the first place. This list in the box on page 56 is pretty extensive, but it can form the basis of a staff meeting to discuss the issues. You can then coordinate their views with your own priorities to create a more positive plan for handling conflict. If you reflect on the numerous discussions and arguments in which you have been involved over the years you will be able to recognise each and every one of the reasons for failure on the list in one or more people involved, including yourself. But don't slash your wrists or jump over the cliff yet—I have also been guilty of almost every one of these shortcomings at some time in my career; in fact, on numerous occasions. The important thing here is to learn from the past and avoid the same mistakes in the future.

In order for grievance procedures to work you need to start by setting up procedures that are open, honest and transparent. Ensure that employees are made fully aware of the procedures and that they understand them. Take the opportunity to focus on the procedures in staff meetings so that individuals and groups will have the confidence to raise issues with the knowledge that the matters will be considered objectively in an open forum. Establish a working environment in which people can work together towards

GRIEVANCE PROCEDURES FAIL BECAUSE:

★ Reasons for a decision are not outlined and the decisions are made without consideration of the facts.

★ Key people are not given the opportunity to present their case.

★ The decisions are inconsistent.

★ The participants change their stories during the process and people withhold vital information.

★ The procedures are conducted away from where the problem occurred.

★ There is a lack of trust in and respect for the other side.

★ There is an inability to crystallise the critical issues from the murky waters of stress and emotion and there are too many hidden agendas.

★ Budget restraints might restrict possible options.

★ Other tasks and functions are given higher priority and policies and procedures are too inflexible.

★ People might be reluctant to be honest for fear of damaging their future prospects, failing or of loss of possession.

★ People are fearful of facing the other party and there is often an imbalance of power, authority or influence between the sides.

★ The procedures are not understood. People are not comfortable with the procedures but are also not confident enough to suggest changes.

★ Some people are not emotionally suited to negotiations.

★ Managers who like to make decisions and get on with it see negotiations as a waste of time. They fear that equity for others could mean a loss of power or influence for them.

★ There is a lack of delegation of authority to make decisions during discussions or otherwise the delegation is unclear.

★ There is too often a desire to protect colleagues at either a managerial or employee level instead of resolving the matter jointly according to the facts.

★ There is a philosophical, professional or cultural opposition to the other side.

★ The reasons for the meeting are unclear or the participants are not given sufficient notice to prepare.

★ There is inadequate research and attention to the facts.

★ There are negative attitudes towards the other side or there is a perceived threat to a person's position.

★ There is inadequate experience and training in the area.

resolving disputes and problems and where these procedures are considered as a normal part of the working environment.

Problems and disputes are a fact of working life; it is what you do about them and how you do it that determines the success of the enterprise. To assure the staff that differences in approach and the conflicts and disputes that emanate from those differences are inevitable in the workplace is a step in the right direction. Develop a culture that accepts that mistakes are made in the most effective organisations but are best resolved by everybody working together. In turn, this atmosphere will reduce the potential for those same mistakes to happen in the future. In such an environment grievance procedures are more of a cooperative effort rather than a hot bed of negative crisis, criticism, guilt and blame.

> *For a period of time I banned the word 'problem' from our workplace. It forced*
> *people to think more laterally and positively. They began to use phrases like:*
>   *'There is a matter I would like to discuss with you . . .'*
>   *'I have a suggestion for improving that area of work . . .'*
>   *'Could the team take time out to discuss this issue?'*
>   *'I have researched some other options for consideration . . .'*
> *The team took great delight in the fact that I had to buy the most number of cakes*
> *for morning tea; the penalty for using the forbidden 'P' word.*

■ ESTABLISHING EFFECTIVE GRIEVANCE PROCEDURES

In small organisations it is often seen as cumbersome to set up formal or structured procedures for the settlement of disputes or for solving problems because almost everyone has visual and verbal contact with everyone else on a day-to-day basis. But even in these organisations there is a need to establish a culture and environment conducive to cooperative problem solving. The size of the enterprise is only one small factor in the scheme of things. In large organisations with greater physical, cultural and professional communication distances there is a definite need to formalise procedures.

Effective grievance resolution does not require a rigid formal approach. In fact, the majority of these procedures are quite informal but they do need to be based on the principles outlined above and the suggestions to follow.

Prepare clear policies and guidelines

Involve a range of people from across the enterprise in the formation and writing of the procedures. Keep it simple and write them in clear language, and remember to provide copies in other languages where appropriate. By keeping the guidelines flexible you will allow for the differences in the people involved and the circumstances that arise.

Make the procedures a regular topic of staff meetings and provide training programs to ensure they are clearly understood. Limit the number of steps in the process and keep it as close to the action as possible. Promote the advantages of in-house resolutions and when a dispute arises allow for normal work to continue as much as possible while the problem-solving process proceeds.

Determine who is to be involved in the grievance

Involve only those people close to the core of the problem. For one reason or another a number of others will want to put in their two bits. It is up to you to decide how appropriate that is to the agreement process and to cull the irrelevant. You may wish to involve the supervisor in charge of that area or a union representative where appropriate.

Invite each of the disputants to have a representative or support person present as a guide and mentor. Encourage the participants to become involved in the problem-solving process as quickly as possible and allow others to assist in the research and information gathering. Allow for a third party to be involved to assist the process as a last resort or at the request of all parties. Ascertain who has the authority to act in these matters.

Determine what is to be negotiated

The critical issues to be considered need to be sorted from the extraneous matters that others wish to place on the table for their own agenda. Once you have clarified the levels of authority, delegation and influence involved in the dispute, you can move on to identifing the extent of the differences and the levels of intensity that the dispute has reached.

The nature of the dispute and the relevance of it to the policies and procedures of the organisation and to the legislation relating to these matters needs to be worked out. What is the relative importance of these matters to the organisation and those operating in it?

Set a timeframe and outline the benefits of handling the matter as quickly as possible before the dispute escalates beyond control. On the other hand outline the benefits of allowing time for accurate research and careful consideration of various options. So from the beginning, outline a timeframe but provide for flexibility as the need arises. In cases of emergency deal with the matter quickly to bring it under control but then allow time to review the longer term requirements to address the conditions that led to the crisis. Regularly review the progress of the timeframe.

Prepare options for consideration

Have the participants prepare a number of options for consideration. Collectively identify the advantages and disadvantages of each option. Even when you do not agree with an option this is a useful exercise because certain advantages of option B and C might be incorporated into option A in the process of coming to agreement between conflicting parties.

In considering the options focus on any aspect where there is agreement. Put those agreements together and try to remould them into a package of resolution. Outline the benefits of coming to agreement and defuse emotional reactions to various options. Clarify the sanctions or penalties that might apply to certain actions or the failure to take action. Eliminate any option that is unlawful or is not permissible within the limits of budgets or policies. Don't waste time on matters that are unlawful or not possible.

Control the progress of the dispute
Determine what conditions will apply during the problem-solving process. As far as possible maintain normal work routines but accept that changes will probably occur after agreement is reached. Ensure that safety and security standards are maintained. Wages and salaries should not be altered during negotiations unless by agreement.

Keep the focus on the agenda and avoid unnecessary distractions. Build up and maintain the momentum towards agreement. For major disputes keep minutes of each meeting and ensure that they include all agreements. Provide copies of these for all participants at each stage.

Reach for agreement
Keep focusing on the need to solve problems, resolve issues and to reach agreement on changes to take place. Highlight and congratulate every effort that results in agreement. Even an agreement in principle will allow for the detail to be sorted out at a later date in a more positive and cooperative environment. Lock down each agreement in the minutes as it occurs. Confirm in the minutes the commitment of all the parties to the actions necessary to put the agreement into practice.

Ensure a follow up to the resolution
Allow time for the agreed changes to take place, but set a timeline for implementation. Ensure that adequate support and training is provided to those who require assistance in implementing the change. Monitor and evaluate the progress of the changes and make any necessary adjustments. Allow for feedback on the success or otherwise of the implementation and regularly meet with the participants to review progress.

Third party intervention
Allow for the use of a third party when special expertise or knowledge is required or when the process becomes locked. Decide whether that third party will act as a mediator, conciliator or arbitrator and outline the procedures that will be adopted if a third party is used.

On the surface this whole process appears to be overly formal and cumbersome and it will not be necessary for the majority of disputes in your workplace. But when you understand the above process it will give you the confidence to deal with more serious conflicts. It will show those around you that you have the ability to deal with critical issues logically, fairly, openly and with due respect to all concerned.

When you can handle the big crises or difficult cases the respect that others have for you will rise dramatically.

Most grievances can be handled on an informal basis within the organisation and become part of the normal day-to-day operations. In some cases they might necessitate the involvement of human resources, senior management, union representatives or organisers when special expertise and experience is required or where decisions need to be made at a higher level. More serious cases or those involving formal awards or contracts will require the intervention of a third party such as a court or tribunal.

Stress the importance of solving problems and resolving disputes in-house as early in the dispute as possible, before the issues have had time to be clouded by emotions and incrimination. It is far better to deal with it in cooperation with the people involved, rather than allow it to be taken out of the environment where the dispute occurred into another setting over which you have little or no control.

Take the procedures outlined above and make them the subject of a staff meeting; or better still, include them in a major training program on conflict–resolution.

■ RECRUITING THE BEST PEOPLE

The selection of the best staff is the most crucial decision an employer can make. The direct and indirect costs of getting it wrong can have devastating consequences for the organisation. Have you ever wondered why so many enterprises have such a high resignation rate and why so many are fearful of the provisions of unfair dismissal? These problems exist because the selection processes have been plagued by patriotism, nepotism, amateurism and ignorance and those selected candidates have lacked the necessary support to ensure job satisfaction and reward in a safe and healthy working environment.

The first principle of recruitment is to select the best person for each job on their merits and to remove all discrimination and harassment from the process. All jobs must be open to all people on the basis of merit. You need to ensure that those involved in the selection process are trained and competent in this crucial area. When you recruit the best personnel your organisation becomes more competitive, there is greater job satisfaction for employees, and there are fewer disputes in the workplace. The best recruits are also more likely to handle progressive change and to contribute to the development of the team and its outcomes.

Start by fully understanding the nature of your organisation. Before recruiting clarify the requirements, accountabilities, roles and responsibilities and the desired outcomes for the vacant position/s. From there identify the personal and professional qualities the person will need for the position. Identify the skills, qualifications and experience necessary to meet minimal standards of performance, safety and quality. Try to select a person who will add to the value of the organisation because of what they bring with them as an individual. Test them to see if they have the ability to work cooperatively in a cohesive team.

On average, workers now change jobs every three to four years. With the pace of change in modern organisations, recruitment is now seen as the most valuable process to bring about strategic change and achieve improved outcomes. Get it right and you will survive in a competitive world; get it wrong and you go under. To select the best people to work cooperatively in a supportive working environment in which they are guided and encouraged to develop their potential, is the surest formula for survival.

To get a balanced, productive and effective employee relations environment, get the recruitment right first.

Try to avoid selecting people with the same qualities and characteristics as yourself as this will result in a static, inflexible situation. When this occurs, stability and status quo are considered as high ideals. In modern organisations, it is more imperative to recruit people with different knowledge, skills, competencies, backgrounds and experiences because they add value to the current pool of talent. Your good supervision and management will tap into and utilise that experience and combine it with the other team members in such a way that the results are greater than the sum of the individuals.

To achieve those ends try to recognise the differences between people; manage the creative tensions between them; encourage their participation in the process; combine them into the most effective teams; provide the necessary support; and resolve the differences that will occur between them. Start by identifying the pool of potential recruits and then attract them towards your organisation. Remember, recruitment is a two-way process; the recruit brings value to the organisation and, in return, the organisation enhances their development and job satisfaction. It is important, therefore, for the enterprise to offer an environment that is attractive to the best candidates. If you feed them peanuts you will only get monkeys. See Activity 10 in Chapter 5.

SUCCESS

There are those who measure the success of recruitment by the number of vacancies filled at the least cost to the organisation. If you are serious about creating a positive employee relations environment then you will consider other factors such as the long-term productivity gains that accrue from those appointments and the quality of their performance. How well will these people fit into, contribute to and add value to the team?

Turnover is another factor to consider in assessing the success of your recruitment program. When you calculate the cost of filling each position, add the cost of induction and the additional monitoring, support and guidance that each new recruit requires. Combine this with the cost of dismissal and any possible pay out if you are unsuccessful. Then look to the interruption to the flow of work or stoppages caused by these changes. Consider the

A SIMPLE READY RECKONER FOR THE RECRUITMENT PROCESS

★ Be clear about the short- and long-term goals of the organisation and be confident in promoting to the candidates your commitment towards achieving them.

★ Determine the values of your organisation or section that you wish to promote—what are you on about and how do you expect to achieve it?

★ Promote the particular qualities and achievements of the section in which the vacancy occurs.

★ Take into consideration the changes occurring in your particular workplace, to the economy in general and to the job market locally and internationally.

★ Conduct a skill-and-job analysis to determine the best mix of positions to meet the needs. Don't just fill a position because it is vacant—determine whether the position will best serve the needs of the organisation. If not, then change it.

★ Be confident about re-designing jobs to suit emerging requirements.

★ Design job specifications with sufficient flexibility to cater for the changing roles, accountabilities, competition and the delegation of responsibility.

★ Identify the pool of potential recruits—whether trainees, apprentices or people to fill senior management positions. Approximately 70 per cent of vacant positions are filled internally or by direct contact with applicants, rather than by open advertising. Consider the wealth of talent that you miss out on when you don't advertise openly.

★ Look to both internal and external pools of talent, including overseas sources. Remember that you want the best. Consider your competitors as well as totally different organisations and industries as sources for recruits. Your staff, customers, unions and professional associations are but a few of the sources who can provide advice.

★ Consider the relative merits of government or private agencies as a pool of talent or for professional advice and input into the selection process.

★ Train key people in the selection process and ensure they are fully aware of legislative requirements.

★ Design the procedures to meet equal employment opportunity, cultural diversity and affirmative action principles and practice. Break down the traditional barriers and restrictions.

★ Construct a package that best recognises and rewards the responsibility of the position and will attract the best candidates.

★ Prepare advertisements or job statements that clearly enunciate the criteria and procedures for selection and determine the coverage of those advertisements.

★ Consider the possible need for skill or other tests, medical reports, criminal records or validation of qualifications.

- ★ Prepare an information package that can be collected, faxed, emailed or posted to potential candidates.
- ★ Determine who is to be involved in the selection and who will make the final decision.
- ★ Decide on short listing applicants and the value of references or referees.
- ★ Conduct the process fairly, openly and honestly, giving each person the opportunity to best present their case and to find out any other information they require.
- ★ Keep accurate records of the process.
- ★ Follow up with unsuccessful candidates—remember, one of them might be your next recruit—and provide developmental advice.
- ★ Ensure the induction of the new recruit is positive, professional, complete and continuous.

costs of grievance or dispute resolution and the hidden costs of low morale, loss of esteem, sabotage, restrictive work practices or strikes that might accrue as a result of an unhappy workplace. Get the selection right in the first place and then concentrate on looking after those quality staff. Then the direct and indirect costs will be considerably reduced.

> **Factor recruitment into your long-term development plans, which may include induction, support, mentoring, training and development, performance feedback and career-path planning.**

Set up on-going assessment of the success of these strategies. Regularly consult with each person in regards to their past performance, their current achievements, their stage of development, their potential and your plans for their future. Blend your assessment with their own assessment and aspirations in reaching positive proposals for their future. When each person feels they are contributing to the value of the organisation while, at the same time, gaining job satisfaction and development, there will be a greater commitment to continue with the organisation and to improve the outcomes to the benefit of all concerned. When the people are recognised and rewarded for those efforts the bonds will be even tighter. See Activity 7 in Chapter 5.

MEASURING EFFECTIVENESS

Having selected the most meritorious people it will now be your objective to retain them and to ensure they work well with their co-workers so that you have the most effective teams. This will be best achieved when you have a planned program of assessment linked to the development of individuals and teams.

Most organisations have in place some variation of a formal performance appraisal system but few of these programs have much to do with enhancing the development of the people involved. They tend to be a formal process whereby people are measured against a prepared list of criteria once or twice a year. Boxes are ticked, general comments are made and the appraisal sheets are filed in the appropriate place. The system is served but little constructive advantages accrue from the process.

> **Planning, tracking, evaluating and developing the work of those who report to you is the most important aspect of your responsibility as a supervisor or manager. You must be willing to spend time with those people.**

Your impact on the development of your staff will peak when the process enhances the dignity and outcomes for each person. Assessment and appraisal are only small parts of a development program. They only provide indicators as to where you should concentrate your training, development and guidance. They are a means to an end, not the end in itself.

Consider first what people want from their work. Job security, satisfactory wages and good working conditions are basic but are not the whole picture. Being trusted, respected, recognised, rewarded and appreciated are high on people's lists and are necessary for the establishment of genuine loyalty. When you provide support, guidance, mentoring, advice and encouragement to the staff they will respond by taking more responsibility, being willing to act independently and contributing to the development of the team.

Staff will respond best when you vary their work to create more interest and provide them with the necessary information, tools and equipment to complete the tasks. Your positive developmental advice will be appreciated when they can see that it leads to the enhancement of their skills and experience and their ability to complete their work effectively. They appreciate open and honest feedback.

Most organisations start with the company mission and goals and develop a common set of criteria to reflect those objectives, then measure everyone on a common set of organisational criteria. It is unrealistic to measure senior management on the same criteria as junior recruits, or the office staff with field officers. To establish an effective performance development program for your staff, first give consideration to each individual in their own right. Look to see how they fit into the team; then measure the success of the team within the context of the organisation. This is a bottom-up model. In this context development is a regular day-to-day, on-going process. (A top-down model is the once-a-year exercise of ticking boxes on the appraisal sheet.) Focus your efforts on providing each staff member with the opportunity for continuous learning and skill enhancement.

Consider some of the following strategies when establishing a positive development program. Encourage the practice of self analysis and peer analysis so that all appraisals are not coming from you. Sit with each staff member and compare and discuss their analysis with yours. They will be even more confident in this process if you are willing to do a 360-degree turn and ask them to analyse your performance. Ask them then to suggest ways in which you and they can better work together for improved outcomes.

Commit yourself to active team development and provide opportunities for staff to be involved in special projects. Vary the combinations in teams from pairs, triples or more. Encourage the pooling and sharing of ideas and resources. When one team member has developed a good method provide each other person with a copy. Promote job rotation and relieving of higher positions on a rotational basis. Encourage staff to regularly assess and review their work patterns and job design. Conduct skills audit to assist the process.

Provide staff with the necessary support, guidance and advice and encourage a planned program of mentoring so that each member will not feel isolated: this way the development is shared across a number of people in the team. Encourage and support action research, initiative and experimentation. Accept that mistakes will be made but they will be best handled through a joint problem-solving approach. Provide demonstrations where necessary to assist the learning process.

When you regularly review the performance of staff look at it in the context of their continuous development. Where have they been? What have they achieved? What have been their experiences? At what stage has their development reached? What do you see as their potential? What further development will be necessary to bring out that potential? What can you do to assist that process? What other experiences or training do they need to continue their progression—both now and in the future? What other advice, support, guidance and mentoring could assist? What opportunities are likely to emerge that could be taken up by this person?

This process will be most effective when you and the staff member collectively analyse their performance and their potential, then agree on a program that best suits them. It will achieve its objectives when it is seen by all as an on-going program and each person is seen first in the context of their own development. When this happens the collective improvement in all of the staff will multiply into a much higher improvement at organisational level because the end result will be greater than the sum of its parts. This is why it is important to work from the bottom up.

■ THE QUESTION OF DISMISSAL

The moment the word dismissal is mentioned anxiety and stress levels rise dramatically, along with arguments of rights and wrongs, fairness and harshness. Employees believe they do not have sufficient protection against unreasonable employers who seem to be focussed on saving costs and pleasing the shareholders. Employers believe the laws are over-protective of workers and that it is almost impossible to dismiss staff. See Activity 8/6 in Chapter 5. This attitude results in too much huffing and puffing and too little action to get the procedure of dismissal right in the first place. Let us now put some common sense into this vexed issue.

If you start by creating a working environment where dismissal is rare, when it has to happen it will be conducted using best practice. To do this:

- ensure your selection procedures identify the best person for a job
- have clear, understandable contracts of employment and job descriptions
- ensure regular training supplements on-going guidance and clear communication
- clearly identify concerns and problems and provide the support necessary to address them
- ensure the working environment is safe and the equipment is well maintained and appropriate for the tasks (and train people properly in the use of that equipment)
- document all serious concerns and the actions taken to assist the person to overcome them.

The legislation surrounding unfair dismissal varies between countries, states and provinces and you should look at the appropriate national and state legislation. But there is a common thread that relates to best management practice. The employer has the right of hire and fire providing they maintain a safe and healthy workplace and they act in a manner that is not harsh, unjust, unreasonable, unfair, unconscionable or unlawful.

When it comes to a legal dispute the various tribunals are not interested in how you organise your operational procedures or sell your product or services. They are only interested in ensuring that everyone is treated fairly and honestly, have been given the necessary support and guidance to perform effectively and that there are good reasons for the dismissal. It is important in dispute–resolution procedures that you have evidence of your concerns and the actions you have taken to address them.

GIVE REASONS

There could be any number of reasons why an employee might be dismissed but you need to look first at the underlying causes—why the situation reached a point where this action had to take place. Consider the background leading up to this point as more important than the surface symptoms of inefficiency, incompetence, incapacity or improper and illegal conduct. Did the original selection process pick this person on merit? Would they have been better placed in another position? Did they have the necessary skills, knowledge and experience to perform satisfactorily? Were they given adequate support and guidance?

There are a number of ways that an employee might be forced to leave. They might be **summarily dismissed** for reasons such as: misconduct, incompetence, incompatibility, physical or verbal abuse, refusal to obey lawful instructions, drunkenness, criminal behaviour, unjustified absenteeism, dishonesty or bribery. When an organisation is being restructured an employee might be forced to take up a position they consider to be unsuitable, and are subsequently forced to resign. Unless they are offered a redundancy this can be considered as **constructive dismissal**. An employee might also be dismissed if their health prevents them from effectively performing the responsibilities of their position, although this matter might involve worker's compensation and superannuation provisions. You should also be aware of the availability of any outside services, such as positive rehabilitation programs, to assist the worker to get back to work.

Most contracts and enterprise agreements these days cover provisions for **redundancy** or **retrenchment**. These occur when an organisation is going through a restructuring process as a result of major changes in competition, supplies, the economy, seasons or technology. The employee is dismissed through no fault of their own. Industrial commissions and courts provide guidelines that include the need for effective communication, consultation, adequate notice, consideration for placement in other positions and the levels of redundancy pay outs.

Retirements and **resignations** are usually arranged by cooperative agreement between the employer and employee and, providing the normal procedures are followed, there are usually no problems in this area. On occasions, these might be arranged by mutual agreement because of the person's inefficiency or incompetence. If, however, the person is forced to resign or retire through coercion, they can proceed with an unfair dismissal application.

INVALID REASONS

Various laws provide protection for employees against the actions of employers, or those acting on behalf of the employer, that are considered harsh, unreasonable and unjust. Employees cannot be dismissed for any of the following:

- temporary absence from work because of sickness, injury or other reasonable cause
- seeking the office of or acting as a union official
- being a union member or refusing to be a union member
- being involved in union activities
- filing a complaint or taking action against an employer in a court of law
- refusing to negotiate or sign a workplace agreement or contract
- taking parental leave
- discrimination on the basis of race, colour, gender, sexual preference, age, disability, marital status, family responsibilities, pregnancy, religion, political opinion, cultural background or language.

Any employee may lodge an application to an industrial commission or court if they feel they have been unfairly treated in regard to their dismissal or have been subject to unlawful actions. In the first place the courts will attempt to conciliate on the matters raised. If you are in this position, on either side of the application, I suggest you seek legal advice as there can be many technicalities to consider in the process.

HOW TO PROCEED TO DISMISSAL

Providing there have been adequate induction procedures, effective communication and positive training and development, then employees guilty of serious misdemeanours may be summarily dismissed. In less serious cases there is a simple process to ensure fairness to all concerned. Many employers argue that the process is time consuming, costly and unfair to them. Some of them give up, believing it is impossible to get rid of an employee no matter what they have done. This of course is untrue and they can achieve their objectives if they follow simple guidelines.

If an employee is performing unsatisfactorily consider the cost to the organisation of not taking the appropriate action. Consider not only the loss of productivity from that person but also the carry-over effect on the loss of faith in the ability of management, low morale, low self-esteem, poor team work, reduced commitment and the development of a negative culture of problems. Start by setting clear guidelines for the support and guidance of all employees to create an environment where there is a culture of joint problem-solving through collaboration. When concerns do arise, deal with them effectively and, if they reach the point of dismissal, handle them fairly, openly and honestly.

When there is a matter of concern, give a warning and provide the necessary advice to allow the person to overcome the problem. Ensure all communications are clear and easily understood and make sure the employee has copies of all relevant documents and reports. In the documents and/or meetings spell out the nature of the problem so there is no mis-understanding. Provide an opportunity for the person to respond to the allegations. If the problem re-occurs provide written advice to the person.

You will need to set up a support program for the employee and put the issues in writing. These should include:

- the issue of concern
- why it is of concern
- what needs to happen to overcome the problems
- what training will be required
- what support will be given and who will provide that support
- the assessment procedures of progress
- a timeline for progress to be achieved
- regular reporting on progress.

You will need to provide reasonable time for improvement to happen and to make sure the person has all the appropriate guidelines, policies and procedures to carry out their work in a satisfactory manner. Stick to the facts and avoid emotional generalisations about the person. Provide the opportunity for the person to explain their actions and express their concerns and allow the person to have representation at any meetings.

It can be an advantage to give a final written warning indicating that dismissal will take place if the required conditions are not met by a stated date. If the conditions are not met and improvement is not satisfactory, then proceed with dismissal. When that takes place call them to a meeting and outline the reasons for the action, including details of the deficiencies or allegations of misconduct. If you have done everything right up to this stage, nothing new should be presented at this meeting. It is merely a final summary of what has happened and a conclusion to the process. At this point you need to provide the person with a dismissal notice in writing, which needs to include the reasons for that dismissal.

When there is a matter of concern make your first objective the resolution of the problems. To do this provide the necessary support to bring the person to a level of effectiveness or to find another position where their skills and experience are better placed. If you have followed these guidelines and improvement does not occur then you can confidently move to dismissal. Appreciate, however, that doing the right thing does not prevent the person from lodging an appeal on the grounds of unfair dismissal. They have the legal right to do so.

If you have to appear at a hearing be certain to take all of the documentation and be willing to explain the process. A commissioner at a tribunal told me that the biggest problems he had in dealing with these cases was that the employer did not follow normal good employee relations practice and did not have any documentation to support their case—not even a dismissal notice. When the guidelines were followed and good practice applied he had no difficulty in dealing with unfair dismissal applications.

■ COMPENSATING FOR INJURY AND ILLNESS

Worker's compensation was designed to protect workers because it was considered that going to work in an industrialised society presented a collective risk that should be shared and guaranteed by all of society. Work is hazardous and the injuries and sickness that result from those hazards should be covered by compulsory insurance. The idea of worker's compensation was initially developed in Britain in the late 1800s and it has been adopted with some modifications by most other Western societies since then. It has further developed from a basic insurance scheme covering people at work into a broader concept of risk management encompassing rehabilitation and occupational health and safety.

Worker's compensation differs from common law in that it is not necessary to prove fault in order to gain compensation. Not even negligence on the part of the worker will prevent the payment for injury, though it might be taken into consideration in determining the level of compensation. Worker's compensation is paid when an injury, death or disease occurs and causes incapacity while the person is at work—operating in the context of work, or travelling to and from work, or in relation to work. This covers people who, under law, are employed under a contract of employment. While it is subject to interpretation, a claim can be made to cover aggravation, deterioration or general worsening of a prior injury or condition.

The claimant must show that an injury or sickness did occur and that it is related to work. There is often reference in claims to 'arising out of, or in the course of employment'. There are some famous cases that stretch the interpretation of this concept but the majority come clearly within its scope. One person was compensated when he was injured at a hotel after work because he claimed that he felt obliged to accept his manager's invitation to have a drink, therefore the injury happened in the context of work. Another claim was an injury sustained while playing squash against the boss on a weekend.

All employers are required by law to have an insurance policy from a registered insurer to cover worker's compensation and rehabilitation. It is important also to ensure that other people, such as contractors who do most of their work with the enterprise, are covered, because they could be deemed to be workers under the terms of the legislation. The worker may claim for a range of benefits, such as weekly payments, to wholly or partly compensate for lost wages, medical expenses, travel expenses, rehabilitation, damage to personal items and compensation for permanent injury. In the case of death, their estate can claim for benefits.

If there is a serious injury at your workplace you should notify the relevant authority. You must submit any claims to the insurer without delay and pass on any benefits immediately to the employee. It is important also to cooperate with the insurer in implementing a scheme of rehabilitation to ease the person back into the workplace. Effective rehabilitation programs are best for both the worker and the organisation and, in the long term, will cost less than paying for a full-time replacement in addition to the extended sick leave. See Activity 8/5 in Chapter 5.

In the past there was too little recognition given to the need for safe and healthy workplaces because employers knew that compensation would be paid regardless of fault. Today, there is more emphasis on the need to have policies and practices of risk management aimed at ensuring a safe and healthy environment. Insurance premiums are very much geared to the relative risk to the workers at your organisation. With the increases in the cost of medical and rehabilitation services, these matters are a significant factor in the annual budget. As accidents and injuries increase the insurance premiums will grow at a greater rate.

You could be held to account for the costs involved in your area as part of your annual budget, and you will soon realise that a safe and healthy workplace is more productive and there are fewer injuries at work. Keep abreast of current trends and gain advice if you are uncertain about these matters. During the 1980s, with the change in the nature and use of technology, there was a proliferation of claims relating to repetitive strain injury (RSI). As a result, there was greater emphasis on the better use of ergonomic furniture and equipment. In the 1990s, with the acceleration in change programs, stress became the flavour of the decade.

Be aware of all safety standards and ensure that workers are provided with reliable equipment and clothing and follow standards of safe behaviour. Severe penalties will accrue if a person is seriously injured as a result of unsafe practices or equipment. See Activity 8/3 in Chapter 5.

You have a personal and professional responsibility for the people who work with you. Don't leave it others, such as the human resources or finance directors. By all means use these people as advisers and experts but I can assure you that your credibility will be highest when you take hold of your own agenda and publicly commit yourself to the support and development of your staff. See Activity 15 in Chapter 5.

chapter 4

Building a better workplace

- How to cope with change

- Maintaining a safe and healthy workplace

- Eliminating discrimination to open up opportunities

- Bargaining an enterprise agreement

- The importance of information systems

As I have argued throughout this book, the development of good employee relations is essential to building a better workplace. In turn, it is essential if you want to improve productivity, effectiveness and competitiveness. You need to see employee relations as part of the big picture and make sure that it is included in major planning and policy decisions and not treated as a series of minor adjustments in the mechanical management of personnel matters. In this chapter we look to the big programs that impact on this critical area.

■ CHANGE MANAGEMENT

Diversity and change are the two most important factors impacting on the good application of employee relations policies and practices. Because change, together with its close partner, conflict, is inevitable and in fact essential to the growth of any organisation, it is imperative to plan for its better management. Change will take place for any number of reasons. In the first place growth and maturity will create change.

> Fred the TV mechanic set up as a sole trader to do repairs. He then expanded and began supplying parts for TVs and employed a partner to look after this area. He saw an opportunity to move into retail so he leased a shop. He employed his wife and daughter to work in the shop, and his son to be an apprentice TV mechanic. With further success he expanded into other electronic equipment and sound systems, and then opened two other stores in neighbouring towns.
>
> At this stage his organisation was getting too large and complicated for him to manage. He employed a manager to look after the organisation of business systems, finance and employee relations. The business was then floated on the stock exchange. With further success there was an opportunity to franchise the organisation on a national basis. At this point Fred was voted out of his position as Chairman of Directors and the organisation expanded into 30 outlets employing 1075 people.
>
> At every stage of the business' development there was considerable adjustment made to the structure and culture of the enterprise. This required significant changes to employee relations, from a simple family enterprise to a large-scale complex organisation.

Changes to the nature of competition and markets will impact on policies and practices. A new strong competitor in the market will make you think more carefully about your cost structures. The nature of your product and service, the demands of your customers and your productivity will change the manner by which you go about your work. There are many examples of how the implementation of technology has changed organisations and employee relations within them. Take banks for instance—how they changed from a people friendly face-to-face operation to one that encourages and almost demands you do your business by impersonal technology. If you want A then press button 1. The implementation of barcode scanning changed the nature of supermarket shopping and the introduction of mobile phones has considerably changed our habits in the past ten years. The growth of tele-marketing and its impact on us has opened up a whole new industry. Changes in government policies and practices, changes in the economic climate, changes in seasons and changes in world alliances all impact on organisations and the need for employee relations to adjust. No matter what you do in the organisation or what position you hold, these changes will affect you. And change will continue to occur.

You have a choice. You can lie back and have it thrust upon you, whether you like it or not, or you can try to participate in that change and therefore have an input into its design and outcomes. The organisation that survives and grows as a result of change has planned for it, knowing that people are essential to successful change management.

Employee relations planning is the vehicle that ensures people can keep up with the momentum of change. Every time you want to implement a change process you need to consider the following matters as essential to the effective outcomes for the employees.

Reasons
Determine first the reasons for change and communicate these clearly to all people concerned.

Research and analysis
Conduct a thorough analysis of the organisation and the particular units that could be affected by the change. This will clarify the need for change, the remedies that will be required and the direction you wish that change to take. You would quickly change your doctor if they prescribed treatment without diagnosis—if they amputated your leg when the symptoms clearly showed you were suffering from a common cold. Likewise it is nonsensical to have a significant restructuring via down-sizing and outsourcing just to eliminate unions and a few difficult members of staff.

People are different
In planning for and implementing change, take into consideration the needs and concerns of each type of person. A person who is excellent in one environment can be a disaster in another. Getting the right combination of people in various project teams is the key to successful change. Here are some categories in which to sort your staff to help you create groups.

- Creative people—are thinkers and dreamers; visionaries who can lift their sights from their navel to beyond the horizon and into the future. They take a more holistic, broad-brush approach and do not feel restricted by detail.

- Analytical people—are excellent at research, planning and the gathering of vital information into orderly patterns. They can restore order out of apparent chaos.
- Action people—will stride over mountains and swim raging rivers to obtain their objectives. They are the risk takers and leaders in implementing change.
- Coordinating people—support the action people by bringing together all of the loose ends and providing the cohesion necessary in a volatile environment of change.
- People people—guarantee that employees are not lost in the exercise. They have a strong sense and understanding of human behaviour and the need to take that into consideration during change.
- Crisis people—quickly move in when conflict or crises occur. They manage these situations with confidence and are comfortable in acting as negotiators, conciliators, arbitrators or mediators. They are excellent in the areas of risk management.
- Rock people—like a safe, stable and secure environment and are the ones most likely to keep the ship on an even keel as it sails through the stormy seas of change. They might be hard to shift from past patterns of operation but they provide an important balance during change.

Commitment

Unless you openly commit yourself to the change process and the reasons for its implementation, then it will not be successful. If the boss is not fully committed why should others waste their time?

Stimulus

The majority of major changes will take place as a result of an external stimulus such as competition, markets, economy, seasons, government, mergers, takeovers or the appointment of a new head from outside the organisation. Try to understand the nature of that stimulus and respond to it.

Culture

Be aware of the values of your current culture and how those might change. Consider the established image you have built up with customers, suppliers, employees and the community. How will that be affected by the change? How might you improve that culture? Sovereignty and loyalty are tested during a period of change. A simple example is I get very suspicious when one of my favourite wines changes its conservative label into an iridescent splash of colour and accompanies the changed image with an increase in price.

Experimentation

It is important for you to encourage open competition between staff members and, where applicable, to combine the creative thinkers so that they might spark off each other. Challenge people to meet and surpass the competition from outside. Don't be afraid to throw your competitors' product on the table for analysis. Challenge the staff to come up with better programs and outcomes.

Corporate knowledge and experience

There are key people in every organisation with an excellent understanding of the corporate culture and how it has developed. They have been involved in past developments and are excellent as mentors to new staff and management and, if encouraged, they can be a boon to the smooth transition to the new order. If discouraged or eliminated they will be a significant loss.

Training and development

For improvements to take place, employees will need to acquire new knowledge and skills. In addition to the regular provisions, budget and plan for all training and development necessary for a smooth change process.

Technology and capital

The acquisition, installation and induction of new equipment will cost time and money that must be written into the equation of change.

Information and communication

If staff don't know, don't blame them for failure. Provide clear information at every stage of the change process and listen to and act upon their responses. Check their understanding. Feedback your response to their suggestions. Keep the flow of information moving.

Realistic scale of change

Most of us can't climb Mount Everest. Be reasonable in your aspirations and set them within the capacity of the organisation and the people to change. It might be more appropriate to plan the changes as a series of small hills to be climbed in sequence, instead of one large insurmountable mountain.

Resources

People assets and other resources must be provided in addition to those required for maintaining the day-to-day operations; certainly during the transition period.

Trust

You will maintain momentum only if you keep the people moving with you and that is best achieved through openness, honesty, transparency, involvement and trust.

Strategies

Clearly identify the means by which the change will take place and who will be involved.

Time

Provide sufficient space for the change to take place, remembering that regular services have to be maintained in the process. Establish clear timelines well in advance so that everyone knows when each stage is to happen and how each person is to be involved.

Mobility

How will the workforce adapt to new positions, responsibilities, locations and team combinations? What provisions have been made for that transfer?

Consultation

Change has a greater chance of success if the people who have to put it into effect are consulted and involved in the development of the proposals and the implementation. Listen to the people around you.

Redesign

Consider the extent to which jobs, work practices and team combinations will require restructuring to meet emerging needs.

Selection

How do you intend to select the best people to occupy new positions in the changed structures?

Outplacement

What provisions have you made to accommodate the outplacement of personnel no longer required in the new structure?

Evaluation

Don't assume that it will work. Select analysts to conduct regular on-going assessment and to suggest modifications. Continuously monitor the implementation to provide the evidence necessary for the next change well in advance and in such a way that the next change will be obvious to most people before it becomes a necessity.

Change can be very positive and it helps the process if you promote it to the staff and others involved. Change can be creative and developmental. It can be dynamic, vital and stimulating. Exploring new horizons can bring the benefits of discovery and empower people to develop their initiative, to implement innovations, to challenge the past and to construct the future. New combinations of people will open up additional opportunities where each team member can learn from others. This in turn will lead to improved personal and professional growth. Change is never easy, but if you follow the guidelines above it is more likely you will have order instead of chaos, and more likely it will have positive outcomes.

It is far better in the first place to recognise the potential of the people and construct an environment in which that can be developed, rather than wait until external pressures make it necessary to change or die. While change is inevitable, it is not continuous; it comes in leaps and bounds with no predictable time between. When you have the most positive and developmental employee relations policies and practices you will be the one that best survives and flourishes in the ambiguity of change.

■ A SAFE AND HEALTHY WORKPLACE

In too many places occupational health and safety is considered to be the responsibility of someone else. Supervisors and managers believe that someone from human resources will look after these matters and that absolves them from responsibility. Nothing could be further from the truth. Everyone is responsible and it is important for you to have a strong commitment, a dedicated program of training and information, a realistic involvement of all employees and an active response to critical issues.

Accept that it is your responsibility to ensure a duty of care for all people associated with your workplace. This will include contractors, suppliers and visitors. Make sure insurance is taken out to cover all workers and set up programs that promote a safe and healthy workplace. When you walk around look for ways to limit the likelihood of accidents, injuries or sickness that could occur at work or in relation to work. Provide and maintain safe systems and work practices by ensuring the safe use, handling, storage and transport of equipment and substances. It is also imperative that everyone associated with the workplace are fully informed and have access to material and training on occupational health and safety matters.

This all relates to the key priority in employee relations—risk management. This will allow you to vary and develop the workplace providing that occupational health and safety remains an integral part of all functions and operations of the organisation. Try to identify hazards and their potential risk, and the means by which those risks will be controlled or eliminated.

Muc-luc Constructions, a house-building company, contracted Tom Martin to complete the roof tiling on their houses because the quality of his work was excellent. The building supervisor told Tom on a number of occasions that it was company policy to observe the provisions of occupational health and safety and it was therefore necessary for him to provide safe scaffolding for himself and others working for him. They knew, however, that Tom never used protective scaffolding unless the house was three levels or higher.

One wet day Harry, one of Tom's workers, fell from the roof breaking bones in his back and sustaining other external and internal injuries when he fell onto a pile of rubbish. He was off work for twelve months and was warned not to work as a roof tiler again.

Although worker's compensation covered the cost of the injuries and time off work, the insurance company took both Tom and the building company to court. The company and Tom had argued that Harry was an experienced tiler, was fully aware of the dangers and should have taken due care and responsibility for his own safety. The insurance company argued that safety procedures for the use of scaffolding on buildings are clearly laid out and that neither Tom nor the company abided by them, and there was a lack of supervision to ensure a safe workplace. The building company's defence was that Tom was a private contractor and responsible for his own team. The court argued that the company was responsible for the site and that Tom was contracted like an employee because most of his work was with that company. The decision was to fine each of them $100 000 for negligence and to fine the building supervisor $5000. It was a very expensive exercise for all concerned, especially Harry, who was incapacitated for life and could not work in the area of his greatest skill and experience.

ESTABLISH AN OCCUPATIONAL HEALTH AND SAFETY POLICY

You will need a written policy that is developed for the whole organisation or your section of responsibility. This will show your commitment to the development of a safe workplace, a necessary pre-condition if any action is taken against you. It tells the world that you and the organisation are serious about safety and welfare and are willing to take responsibility for it. People are more productive, cooperative and positive when they know their employer is committed to ensuring a safe and secure workplace and that their welfare is a high priority.

Constantly remind everyone of the high value you place on the maintenance of standards of occupational health and safety and support this with best practice and supervision in the workplace. Regularly consult with staff to include their suggestions in policies and procedures. Include in your policy outline who is covered by the policy, the responsibilities of all concerned, the establishment of occupational health and safety committees and the nature and extent of training and development in this area.

To show you are serious about your duty of care, seriously consider the following:

- accept your responsibility for this important area—don't pass it on to someone else
- read the relevant legislation and regulations relating to your workplace and practices
- actively walk around your workplace and evaluate the safety of equipment and procedures
- act quickly to remedy any problems

- promote a culture of care and delegate responsibilities to everyone around you
- identify and provide welfare and health facilities for workers who are injured and can be rehabilitated
- ensure that everyone has access to information and is trained in the use of hazardous materials and equipment
- provide on-going monitoring of work practices and equipment to ensure safe standards
- keep accurate records relating to the safety and health of all employees
- provide training for all workers on these matters
- ensure that all signage and information is in a language that is easily understood by all.

See Activity 9 in Chapter 5.

SET UP REPRESENTATIVE COMMITTEES

Occupational health and safety committees provide a forum for management and employees to get together on a regular basis to develop policies and make any necessary modifications to ensure a better environment of safety. A majority of workers should vote to have such a committee and make a submission to the employer or management. Committee members should be elected by the employees and, if possible, will represent the various sections. These committees can make an impact by:

- providing vital information
- identifying potential hazards
- inspecting and assessing the workplace
- helping to solve safety and welfare issues
- assisting with training and development
- assisting with the writing of policies and procedures
- making recommendations to management
- researching new approaches
- consulting with other workers.

The prime objective of these committees is to assist you to develop a safe working environment—one in which the emphasis is on the prevention of injury and sickness and one that will respond quickly when incidents occur. It is advisable to appoint committee members, or others as contact persons, or OH&S representatives, from the various sections of the workplace. Inexperienced employees and those who are less confident are more likely to talk about issues and problems with someone from their own section than go to senior management with a complaint.

PROVIDE TRAINING AND DEVELOPMENT

Ensure that all committee members, supervisors and managers attend a training program on occupational health and safety. Some might consider this to be a boring and tedious exercise, especially when they work in places such as offices and shops where the perceived risks are fewer. The alternative is to walk in ignorance and then find yourself in court trying to justify any inaction that led to a serious injury or the death of one of your colleagues.

Include occupational health and safety in your regular staff meetings and gradually include all staff in training programs in this area. Remember that new staff members were not present when any initial programs were conducted, therefore it is important to include occupational health and safety in all induction programs. Training should also focus on providing all the necessary skills and knowledge for the use of all newly acquired equipment and machinery.

PROVIDING REALISTIC MANAGEMENT

It is important for you to deal with occupational health and safety issues as they arise every day. Acting and reacting to safety issues and responding to problems, injuries and sicknesses is your high priority. Once clear policies are formulated in conjunction with staff and supervisors, and managers or staff members have been appointed to be responsible for specific health and safety issues you can then remind every person to accept their responsibility in this area. Ensure each person understands that responsibility.

Contact your local authority to clarify your legal responsibility and respond immediately to a notice of concern. Design and construct the best working environment to ensure the safe usage of all equipment, machinery and technology. Remove all hazards and provide the necessary safe storage and protection from them. Use safer methods and materials, ensure effective ventilation of your premises, identify, assess and control risks and educate the staff on matters in relation to occupational health and safety.

You need to deal with risks and stresses related to workplace layout and design, manual handling, repetitive strain injuries, plant and equipment, mobile vehicles, noise, sunlight, skin disorders, cancer, smoking, asbestos, mineral fibres, infectious diseases, sexual harassment, assault, drug abuse, domestic violence, fire and hazardous substances. This might seem daunting but the provision of protective equipment and clothing and the confidence that everyone knows how to operate equipment safely is not that difficult to implement. Simply clarify emergency procedures and train key people in first aid as well as providing the necessary materials to support them.

Encourage participation by those affected in rehabilitation programs aimed at getting people back to work. Develop a range of strategies such as job redesign, job rotation, job sharing, mentoring and team development, to make the work place more interesting and supportive and to increase job satisfaction. And, most importantly, constantly review and modify practices.

Margaret Jackson, a senior supervisor, was concerned with the efficiency of Catherine Morris and set up a program of support, regular review and follow-up. She was careful to document all matters and ensured that Catherine was linked with Andrew Downs, a very experienced, understanding and supportive person in the unit. She encouraged the union representative to be present at all meetings so that Catherine had access to further advice.

After a period of two months there was little or no improvement in Catherine's efficiency and Elizabeth Campbell, the human resources manager, was called in to conduct a review of the processes. She suggested some additional strategies that were implemented with Catherine's agreement. After another two months Margaret advised Catherine that she was inefficient and that she was going to recommend her dismissal. When Elizabeth Campbell called Catherine to a meeting to discuss her efficiency, Catherine went to her doctor who then claimed that Catherine was suffering from stress brought on by the pressures exerted by her supervisor and human resources manager. Each time Catherine returned to work and was called to a meeting she again went on stress leave.

What would you do in this situation? My advice is to check that all of the procedures were followed and that the support and guidance was provided for Catherine. Look to the option of placing her in other positions that might better suit her skills and experiences. Document all procedures and provide copies to all concerned. When you have ensured that everything has been done correctly you may proceed with dismissal, but not while Catherine is on sick leave. Wait until she returns. See Activity 9 in Chapter 5.

■ DISCRIMINATION EQUALS LACK OF OPPORTUNITIES

In Chapter 2 we briefly mentioned the relevant legislation relating to this important area. Before you try to program it into the workplace you need to understand the terminology.

Discrimination

This occurs when a person is treated unfairly because they have a particular characteristic that is deemed undesirable by another person. It could be their gender, pregnancy, race, colour, ethnic background, religion, union membership, political association, nationality, language, marital status, sexuality, disability, age or a physical characteristic.

Direct discrimination occurs when someone is treated unfairly because they belong to particular groups such as migrants or Aboriginal people. Some employers refuse to employ anyone who is a union member. Indirect discrimination occurs when the organisation sets conditions that deny the opportunity for certain people to be considered. A job advertisement that specifies criteria such as a height of 185 centimetres, a weight of

90 kilograms and an ability to lift weights of 60 kilograms will discriminate against most women, many men and many ethnic groups. An advertisement that requires applicants to be 25 to 35 years of age discriminates against older people.

Equal employment opportunity

Equity and equal access to opportunities ensures that employees are given a fair chance when applying for jobs, employment conditions, training and development and promotion. Everyone does not have the same skills, knowledge or experiences but they must be given an equal opportunity to demonstrate what they have in open competition with others and be treated fairly and honestly in the process. They have a right to equal access to information and support in those processes.

Affirmative action

There is general agreement that certain groups and minorities have been discriminated against in the past. Women, indigenous people and certain ethnic groups would fall into this category. Legislation in this area allows for strategies to be put in place to assist groups who have been affected by past practices and policies. Special training programs might be given to indigenous people or migrants from a non-English speaking background. Special consideration might be given to attempt to restore the imbalance of women in management positions.

If you have watched the Paralympics you will realise that the competitors are elite athletes who happen to have a restriction that limits their performance. These people still fall into the top 20 per cent of athletes in the world and certainly show the same or better levels of training and commitment as other athletes in this category. All they ask for is the opportunity to compete and be recognised for their achievements. Employees with disabilities ask for the same consideration and, in most cases, it will require some minor, reasonable adjustments to be made to access, equipment and furniture in order for them to perform on an equal footing with others. Give them the opportunity and they will more than repay your consideration.

Harassment

Harassment is any form of behaviour that is uncalled for, not wanted or asked for and embarrasses, humiliates, intimidates or offends another person. It is not confined to acts of a sexual nature, although those cases have the higher public profile. In addition to the discriminatory factors listed the following would qualify as harassment:

- the distribution or display of material or publications that are racist, sexist, sexually explicit or homophobic
- the telling of sexist jokes or those based on a person's gender, pregnancy, race, homosexuality or disability

- separating or not considering people because of their particular characteristics
- verbal or physical abuse aimed at particular stereotypes or individuals who have those characteristics.

See Activity 8/2 in Chapter 5.

WHAT DO YOU NEED TO DO?

Your first objective to handling discrimination is to develop a working environment in which each employee is treated with respect in an open, honest and fair manner. Encouragement is given to each person to perform to the best of their ability; therefore they will have equal access to training and job opportunities. Recognise their work and reward them without bias or favouritism, and ensure they will not be subject to discrimination because of their particular characteristics.

> *Louise Hall, while on maternity leave, was replaced by a casual employee. A week before her intended resumption of duty she was told that her services were no longer required because the person who replaced her was doing an excellent job and it was considered that her additional responsibilities of looking after the new baby would limit her performance at work. It was also anticipated that she would require more leave when the child became sick. After conciliation at an anti-discrimination tribunal Louise accepted a substantial financial compensation.*

To establish your workplace as one where everyone is treated fairly and has equity of opportunity ensure your workplace has a written policy regarding the fair treatment of employees. Check other policies and procedures to ensure that they are non-discriminatory. Apply the same standards and expectations to all employees. Be consistent in your decisions and in your behaviour. You should not be harder on any particular person or group nor show favouritism to particular friends, relatives or associates.

> *A former associate of mine would often ask a friend to apply for a vacant position with the promise that, if they did so, they would be guaranteed the job. This action discriminated against and eliminated others with greater merit.*

Try not to assume that certain groups act or can't act in certain ways. For example you can't assume that more mature people aren't active, vital and dynamic as implied in some advertisements aimed at young people. Likewise, women should not be denied the opportunity to work in areas requiring the lifting and movement of materials. With the use of good equipment they could be more effective and less susceptible to injury than a man using muscle.

All your selection procedures must be based on clear criteria that have the best chance of being assessed in relation to the job responsibilities. Be careful that tests, references and qualifications are not flavoured by discrimination. Ensure that interviews are conducted in a fair manner where each candidate has an equal chance of presenting their case. Check that your decisions do not indirectly discriminate against any person. For example, seniority is no longer an acceptable criteria for selection; merit is.

Try to accommodate the needs of religious groups in the same way that we recognise Easter and Christmas for Christians. Do not insist that English be spoken at all times if this is not necessary for effective performance. Check that your decisions are fair and are communicated in a form that is easily understood by all. It might be necessary, especially in regard to safety issues, to prepare policy documents and signs in other languages.

Make yourself available so that others will feel comfortable coming to you with concerns. It is better to hear about problems early when they are easier to manage than be kept in the dark until they become major crises. On receipt of an allegation of discrimination, improper conduct, harassment or crime, act quickly and in accordance with policies, procedures or the law as appropriate. Do not make assumptions about the complainant.

> 'Oh, not you again Mary. I am sick and tired of listening to your constant stream of complaints. If you put all your effort into doing your job instead of whingeing we wouldn't have any problems. You are a virago of ill tidings. Go away.'

Remember that Mary, this time, might be here to tell you that the building is on fire and about to fall down.

Establish codes of conduct that are promoted by your own behaviour. Project the image that this workplace values good working relationships where discrimination and harassment are not tolerated and where everyone is treated equally on the basis of merit. Constantly monitor the workplace and listen for the vibrations. Tune into the responses of those around you. Be sensitive to the early indicators of concern. Move in to fine tune the operations and patterns of work in response to those vibrations. I suspect you cannot do that successfully from the confines of your office, behind closed doors, while playing with your emails. Get out and about until you can see the whites of their eyes. Don't be afraid; they are only people. And you might find it interesting and rewarding.

■ THE ENTERPRISE AGREEMENT

Enterprise agreements, workplace agreements and contracts aim to set out conditions of employment that have been agreed to by the employer and the workers. They differ from awards in that they apply to particular types of work in one enterprise or project rather than a whole industry. They are negotiated voluntarily by the employees and the employer. The workers can use a consulting committee or union to act on their behalf. The following suggestions will apply as much to the development of enterprise agreements as they will to the negotiation of individual contracts. The principles are the same, only the scale is different—regardless of which side you are on.

When you are formalising an enterprise agreement or employment contract ensure it meets minimum requirements relating to such matters as leave, dismissal, wages, freedom of association, superannuation and worker's compensation. These matters cannot be negotiated away in return for other benefits. Make sure the agreement was not signed under duress and that there was adequate information available to all the parties to make a considered decision. There should also have been adequate consultation on these matters, the workers should not have been denied access to support, and there should have been a clear understanding of the conditions included.

■ THE MAJOR STEPS IN ENTERPRISE BARGAINING

1. Representation

Determine the people or groups that will be covered by this agreement or contract and identify those who will represent each of the interested groups. There might be one or a number of trade unions representing the employees or alternatively, the employees might have no unions so they might represent themselves, get other expert support or elect by secret ballot a representative committee to act on their behalf. Employers might call upon their association or use legal advice. Clarify whether the agreement affects one or a group of workers, whether they are involved with a particular project, trade or profession or whether it is all encompassing for everyone in the enterprise.

2. Negotiation

Decide first the manner by which negotiations will proceed—whether as an on-going consultative committee or a one-off process. Select an environment that promotes an atmosphere of openness, trust and honesty and is mutually agreed upon by all concerned. Ensure effective communication by the sharing of information and that all people affected are fully informed throughout the process.

It is preferable that all concerned are trained in negotiation strategies and understand the process. The negotiators involved will be more effective when they are well prepared and have a good understanding of the enterprise. Those who understand that the process does not end with the signing of the agreement will have a greater commitment to ensuring that its provisions are implemented after the event. These people are more likely to bargain in good faith.

3. Drafting the agreement

In reality, most agreements are prepared in draft form by one party and worked on by both sides until agreement is reached. In doing so, convoluted and ambiguous language or too much legalese is avoided. Write the document in plain English that can be easily understood by all concerned. Be mindful of the audience and constantly test the understanding of what is written. What might be very clear to you might not be to others, and statements might be interpreted in a number of different ways. Explain technical terms where necessary. Later I discuss what can be included in the agreement and you can use this list as a guide to set out the agreement in clear sections. Remember to allow space for the signatories to the agreement.

4. Checking

Enterprise agreements, especially for large-scale enterprises, can involve very complicated processes and it is therefore advisable to have the agreement checked by independent parties before signing. Some government authorities will check to see whether the agreement meets statutory requirements such as anti-discriminatory legislation. You might like to consult either an employer association or a union for assistance. Private consultants, lawyers or accountants might also be of assistance.

5. Acceptance by employees

If the employees are not represented by a union then it is necessary for those workers to conduct a secret ballot to determine if there is agreement to its terms or whether it is necessary to vary the provisions, or terminate the agreement.

6. Commitment to the agreement

For an enterprise agreement or contract to have legal status it must be signed by or on behalf of all parties. This might include all employees covered by the agreement, trade unions representing the employees, a representative committee, a single employer, a group of employers, employers combined in a special project or an employer association representing the employer.

7. Registration

It is best that any enterprise agreement is registered with an industrial commission or government authority. This will add another layer of checks and balances and ensure that it meets the minimum requirements set down in various pieces of legislation. It will also ensure that the workers have not been forced under duress into signing. They will also consider such matters as whether the agreement is in the public interest and that the conditions agreed upon are not disadvantageous in relation to the former agreement or award that it replaces.

DIFFICULTIES YOU WILL FACE

If you become involved in the process of enterprise bargaining, especially in large-scale organisations, realise that it can be very difficult and time consuming. There are barriers that affect the negotiation process and some of these are listed below. Try to anticipate these hurdles and develop in advance strategies to address them.

Too little knowledge of the process

Get information from your industrial relations departments and have experts in this area conduct training for all concerned, especially for supervisors, managers and worker representatives on consultative committees.

Fixation on traditional methods

There is often a lack of appreciation that the traditional wage cases and centralised procedures no longer apply except for minimum wage determinations. Educate all concerned participants in the latest principles and processes of enterprise bargaining.

Imbalance of power and influence

Identify avenues for support and guidance, such as employer associations, professional associations, solicitors, accountants, or private consultants. Ultimatums that insist on acceptance will always create further tensions.

Inadequate confidence in negotiations

Read the book *Making Negotiations Happen* from this series and seek advice and support from others more experienced than yourself. Negotiators need to have the power and authority to make decisions in order to be effective.

Over emphasis on wages and salaries

This can happen to the detriment of other matters in the package. Consider the list on page 90 of all matters that might be considered in coming to an agreement.

Over emphasis on cost cutting

This could be to achieve greater efficiency instead of stressing the broader dimensions of productivity improvements through more effective work practices.

Inadequate consultation

Encourage the establishment of consultative committees that meet regularly as an ongoing procedure. Promote the principle of joint problem solving.

Poor communication

This can be a major stumbling block and lack of feedback to the relevant parties inhibits positive progress.

Lack of trust and respect

There is a fear that unions will disrupt proceedings through industrial action. From the other side, the fear is that employers will use their coercive power to force through provisions that are to the disadvantage of workers. In the first place, bring in support to assist your presentation. Then consider the use of a facilitator or, as a last resort, have the matters arbitrated.

Inadequate time given to preparation

The process of researching and writing proposals so that you can present your case, consider your alternatives and draw up agreements, takes time. Remember to allow adequate time.

WHAT CAN BE INCLUDED?

The following is a long list of items that can be included in an enterprise agreement. This list is not all inclusive and can vary according to the particular circumstances of your organisation or project team. By starting with these points, however, you will at least have something concrete from which to work. There will be many matters, such as leave provisions, for which there will be no disagreement and therefore can be resolved quickly. Other issues will require different levels of discussion—certainly when it comes to increases in wages and salary on one side and demands for increased productivity on the other.

While working through these matters focus on the individual item but keep an eye on the total picture. This way you will be able to spot an area where a trade off on one issue can be made in the light of movements in others. The best negotiators are like champion team players in sport. They not only look to where they are going to pass the ball, they turn 360 degrees in order to assess the total team play across the field.

Go through the following list and indicate on a scale of 1 to 5 the relative importance of the issues for you, acting as the responsible negotiator. Then do the same exercise as if you were representing the other side in the discussions. Finally, rank them according to the perceived difficulty in the negotiations.

WE'RE AGREED!

Once the agreement is signed and registered it will take effect. The agreement can be terminated at any time with the consent of both parties, but will generally remain in force until another agreement is formulated, signed and registered, even if it goes beyond the stated fixed term. Each agreement contains provisions for grievance procedures should there be disputes with the application or interpretation of the terms of the agreement.

To overcome the overwhelming impact of torrid enterprise bargaining procedures every two to three years it is best to set up joint consultative committees that meet regularly throughout the period of the agreement. It is more likely then that the next round of

Figure 4.1

★ Principles underlying the agreement—philosophy, mission or vision, commitment to quality management, productivity and efficiency, and duty of care towards employees.			
★ Coverage—people who come within the umbrella of this agreement.			
★ The award or agreement that this replaces			
★ Places of employment covered by this agreement			
★ Consultation, both with individuals and joint consultative committees			
★ Communication and confidentiality of information			
★ Classifications, skills and qualifications			
★ OH&S—welfare, first aid and rehabilitation of injured workers			
★ Counselling and disciplinary procedures			
★ Dismissal, stand down, redundancy, retrenchment and retirement			
★ Protective equipment and clothing			
★ Grievance procedures			
★ Performance management and appraisal systems			
★ Locality, travel and other special allowances			
★ Supply of tools, equipment and technology			
★ Hours of work—starting and finishing, overtime, meal breaks, weekend work, public holidays, flexible hours, rostered days off and availability for on call for emergencies			
★ Wages and salaries—including payment, classifications, rates of pay, taxation, part time, temporary, casual, permanent, penalty rates and overtime			
★ Salary packages and allowable arrangements			
★ Superannuation			
★ Insurance			
★ Leave provisions—including annual, public holidays, sick leave, long service, bereavement, study, carers, compassionate, maternity, paternity and jury service			
★ Childcare facilities			
★ Provisions for working from home			
★ Training and skill development—including sabbaticals, job rotation, job redesign, competency based training, formal education, acquisition of additional qualifications, career-path planning, multi-skilling, broad banding and skills auditing			
★ Provisions for restructuring—including consultation, redundancies, retrenchments and job re-classifications			
★ Fixed term of this agreement			
★ Recognition that it meets the statutory requirements			
★ Signatures of people representing the parties to the agreement			

negotiations for a new agreement will be smoother because both groups will come to the table better informed and more experienced in negotiation.

If you are negotiating a personal contract ensure that you look for indicators of your terms of employment. Check whether the contract is for you as a sole trader or as an employee, and whether you are responsible for your own taxation, insurance and super-annuation. If you are responsible for those matters check how these conditions are balanced by better rates of pay and conditions to compensate.

■ INFORMATION SYSTEMS

Traditionally, organisations have been responsible for keeping accurate records of employees. In the past these have been confined to personal and professional information and records of payroll. In today's rapidly changing environment it is now more important to take a strategic approach to management. This means you need to ensure that the information systems about employees provide the relevant data to assist strategic management and action plans and to facilitate the day-to-day operations of the enterprise. This will ensure that employees will benefit from their entitlements and that performance and productivity can be accurately assessed, as well as providing the necessary information from which changes can be made.

It is no longer acceptable for human resources' systems to be confined to the human resources specialists. It is imperative that all supervisors and managers are fully conversant with systems and have access to vital information that will assist them in daily planning and operations. The better the information, the better able the organisation will be to meet the challenges of globalisation, increased competition, changed management, downsizing, outsourcing and restructuring. Human resources' systems will be the best when they are integrated into the overall strategies of the enterprise and become part of the vital information on which budget decisions are made.

With advances in technology it is now possible to maintain very sophisticated systems. You will need to decide which is best for you based on the size and complexity of your organisation, and by identifying all the relevant information about employees you will need to put into operational units from which it is easy to enter or retrieve data on an individual or group basis. But remember the overriding importance of who has access to that information, is the need for privacy and confidentiality, the quality and usefulness of data and ethics.

Human resource information systems are only as good as the people who manage and operate them. The system is there to serve the people in the organisation, not the other way around.

In the early days, data systems related almost exclusively to payroll but more recently this has broadened into a more holistic approach to people management as part of an

Personnel data

Select from the following list those matters you believe are appropriate to your organisation.

personal details	education	training
qualifications	prior service	payroll
benefits	allowances	hours
permanent/part time	position	section
location	enter on duty	termination
religion	language	disability
dependents	next of kin	contacts
medical	professional associations	proficiency level
deductions	transfers	promotions
leave record	banking	superannuation
special issues	performance appraisal	bonuses

organisational management and strategic planning process. Some still see payroll exclusively as an accounting function separate to employee relations, but they are generally protecting their traditional territorial rights rather than implementing good and effective management.

People who take the traditional approach of personnel management are like the employees in a mechanical pipe factory. They see their function merely as supplying pipes of various sizes. Those of you who take an employee relations approach act more like the managers who see their organisation as a producer of liquid-flow systems, consisting of integrated parts that work in harmony to produce successful flows. In the latter it is easier to coordinate and transfer from one section to the other because the individuals don't see themselves as isolated—they see themselves as contributing to the whole. You can as plan more successfully when you can see the forest as well as the individual trees.

Organisational needs

Before deciding on the relevance of data to be collected look to the organisational needs.

training and development	performance management	recruitment
strategic planning	budgeting	occupational health and safety
risk management	selection processes	auditing
job analysis and design	equal employment opportunity	human resources planning
career planning	employment projections	benefits
environmental analysis	turnover	attrition
rosters	tracking applicants	

MAINTAINING THE SYSTEMS

Ensure that records contain accurate, comprehensive information about the employees and pay due regard to privacy and confidentiality. Establish systems that are flexible, dynamic and adaptable to meet emerging needs. Have sufficient space and power for future variations and add ons. Organise information in modular units that can be easily coordinated or presented in a variety of integrated combinations.

Give consideration to freedom of information and priority to quality information, allowing for the easy elimination of irrelevant data. Allow for the effective management and development of employee relations issues. Provide relevant information to all people who have a need for it and have the authorisation to use it. Provide easy access to information in a format that serves your purposes. Many systems are good at data entry but are suspect when it comes to data retrieval. It is necessary to determine first what individual information and what reports are required and in what format, for whom, and for what purpose.

In designing or purchasing a system it might be difficult to decide on its limits. No system represents all things to all people and there are boundaries as to what it can and can't do. You will be crowded by sales people who will want to sell you technology that will take you to Jupiter, Saturn and Neptune first class and be back in time for breakfast. But you don't need that for an organisation with 200 people. Ensure that each function, such as payroll, leave or recruitment is effective in its own right but at the same time can be coordinated with other factors for strategic purposes, evaluation and planning. It will be necessary to have sufficient detail and capacity to be meaningful to the operators but, at the same time, not be so complex that it restricts its use.

Have people trained in the operations of the system to ensure it will serve the organisation and not the other way around. Employee relations is the highest priority and the technology is there to facilitate. By saying that I do not underestimate the importance of technology to this process but it should be seen in the context of other priorities. On the other extreme there are too many organisations still managing human resources systems with a chalk-and-slate approach and some have even run out of chalk.

There are many systems from which to choose. Look to similar size industries and enterprises. Talk to employees and managers who have worked elsewhere. Seek advice from union representatives or employer associations. Read professional magazines. Bring in consultants. Contact a number of known computer systems organisations on an obligation-free basis for advice. Ask them to show you their systems and their practical applications.

Some organisations are now outsourcing their human resources systems to specialist enterprises. Before you consider this option, do a thorough analysis and compare it with the alternative of training good people internally to do the same job. Managing employee relations does not necessarily require people who are human resources specialists, although this can be a distinct advantage. Primarily it requires people with good management skills, who are intelligent, dynamic, vital, who have good problem-solving skills and can deal with crises. They will be able to think clearly on their feet and not be afraid to make decisions. They will understand the complexities of human behaviour, be compassionate to special needs but will have the courage, confidence and foresight to forge through the clouds of emotion, stress and panic to reach their clear objectives. Give me such a person and I will teach them the technicalities of employee relations in a week or two.

See Activity 15 in Chapter 5.

chapter 5

Activities

What will you bring to my organisation?

In this rapidly changing world we all have to face the reality that we will change jobs more often than in the past. This will not only affect you personally but you will also be more involved in the recruitment and selection of others. Therefore, it is important to sharpen your skills of people analysis and to assess what others will bring to your organisation. To start, practice on yourself. Below is a list of criteria an employer might look for when placing a person in a position of responsibility. Rate yourself on a scale of 1 to 5 (with 5 being highest) according to each of the criteria. You can then use this form to rate candidates you are interviewing.

Desirable attributes	1	2	3	4	5
Leadership	☐	☐	☐	☐	☐
Communication skills (written, verbal, technological)	☐	☐	☐	☐	☐
Interpersonal and people skills	☐	☐	☐	☐	☐
Logical reasoning and thinking skills	☐	☐	☐	☐	☐
Problem-solving skills	☐	☐	☐	☐	☐
Risk and crisis management skills	☐	☐	☐	☐	☐
Decision-making skills	☐	☐	☐	☐	☐
Ability to build teamwork	☐	☐	☐	☐	☐
Capacity to work independently	☐	☐	☐	☐	☐
Initiative, creativity and planning skills	☐	☐	☐	☐	☐
Ability to coordinate and administer	☐	☐	☐	☐	☐
Evidence of continuous learning	☐	☐	☐	☐	☐
Involvement in training and development	☐	☐	☐	☐	☐
Ability to meet deadlines	☐	☐	☐	☐	☐
Willingness to be flexible and adaptable	☐	☐	☐	☐	☐

What do you believe to be your main strengths?

_____

_____

_____

_____

What do you intend to do in the next year to further enhance your skills and development and to close the gap on any shortcomings?

_____

_____

_____

_____

On what special projects have you worked in the past three years?

_____

_____

_____

_____

What have been your major achievements during that period?

_____

_____

_____

_____

In what ways have you added value to and improved productivity in the organisations in which you have worked in the past three years?

_____

_____

_____

_____

Summarise the reasons why you are ready to take on the responsibilities of this new position in this dynamic, progressive enterprise for a package that most people would die for?

_____

_____

_____

_____

Research has identified a number of strategies that are used by people to influence others. The list below is a brief summary of those strategies. Circle the ones you use most often at work to influence others and write beside it how you use it and how might you change your approach.

Logical reasoning _____
_____

Creativity _____
_____

Personality, charisma _____
_____

Interpersonal skills _____
_____

Communication skills _____
_____

Listening and responding _____
_____

Providing feedback _____
_____

Planning and developing _____
_____

Negotiating, mediating, conciliating _____
_____

Problem solving _____
_____

Friendliness _____
_____

Kindness, compassion _____
_____

Building teamwork _____
_____

Providing support and guidance _____
_____

Constructing plans _____
_____

Presenting ideas

_____
_____

Assertiveness

_____
_____

Using status and higher authority

_____
_____

Being directive

_____
_____

Being coercive

_____
_____

Demanding

_____
_____

Threatening, blaming, shaming

_____
_____

Assaulting

_____
_____

Withdrawing

_____
_____

Using sanctions and penalties

_____
_____

You are about to be interviewed by your boss for your annual review. Before that you will need to analyse your own effectiveness so that you are able to discuss your performance from a position of knowledge and clarity based on factual information. In preparation for this interview answer the following questions.

During the past year:

What have been your main achievements?

What value have you added to the organisation?

How have you assisted in developing a better working environment for those around you?

What have you done to improve your professional development through training and education and how have you broadened the scope of your skills, knowledge, understanding and experience?

In which areas have you met or exceeded the targets set at the beginning of the year?

In which areas did you not meet the targets and expected outcomes?

What reasons (not excuses) can you put forward for not meeting targets?

What could you have done differently that might have improved these areas?

What other factors beyond your control influenced the outcomes?

_____

_____

_____

_____

_____

_____

_____

_____

In the year ahead:

What have you been doing well that you will continue to do?

What new approaches have you tried that are proving to be valuable strategies and will be extended in the future?

Which strategies are losing their impact and will be used less frequently in the future?

Which aspects of your work have little value and will be dropped from your program?

What new approaches would you like to implement next year?

What are the costs and implications of these initiatives?

How will you change your approach to enhancing the working environment for the people in your area of influence or responsibility?

_____

_____

_____

_____

_____

_____

_____

Your development

How do you see your current stage of development?

Where would you like to be in one, three and five years time?

What has to happen to achieve those aspirations?

What do you have to do to enhance your potential and to achieve greater job satisfaction?

What do you see as the emerging opportunities to enhance or broaden your development?

_____

_____

_____

_____

_____

_____

_____

Now consider how you intend to present this self-analysis to your boss when you discuss your future.

_____

_____

_____

_____

_____

_____

_____

For this exercise, assume you are being offered an individual contract for two years. You will need to negotiate the terms with your prospective employer. Answer the questions below and fill in your responses. When you fully appreciate this process as it affects you, you will then be in a better position to understand it from the candidate's point of view when you are hiring for a position.

Questions to ask yourself	Your response
What research will you need to do before you go to the bargaining table?	
Where can you gain further information?	
Are there any other people or organisations that might assist you?	
How will you present your case?	
What approach do you anticipate from your employer?	
How will you prepare for that anticipated approach?	
What will be your ambit claim or wish list?	
How will you justify your requests?	
What do you believe will be the reaction to your requests?	
How will you respond to those reactions?	
What do you believe will be the counter offer from your employer?	

What improvements in productivity can you offer to offset a better package?	
Is there anything you are willing to sacrifice or exchange in order to gain other benefits?	
What would you see as a healthy balance between your demands and the expectations of your employer?	
How close to that healthy balance do you expect the final agreement to be?	
What must you do to maintain the momentum towards achieving the balance of those outcomes?	
What major changes to your position, roles, responsibilities, accountabilities or location will you propose?	
What suggestions or requests will you make for your own professional development or training?	

You have probably been involved in a number of major changes or restructures in your organisation over the past few years. Consider a major change process in which you have been involved recently. The following elements are essential for successful change management. Rate each of them on a scale of 1 to 5 (5 being highest) according to the degree of priority you gave them in that change. After you have rated the elements, consider what would you change if you had to do it again.

CHANGE ELEMENT	1	2	3	4	5
The reasons for change had credibility and were communicated clearly	☐	☐	☐	☐	☐
Research and analysis was conducted beforehand	☐	☐	☐	☐	☐
People differences were considered	☐	☐	☐	☐	☐
There was a genuine commitment from top- and middle-management	☐	☐	☐	☐	☐
The stimulus that promoted the change was well understood	☐	☐	☐	☐	☐
Consideration was given to the value of the culture of the organisation and how it might be affected by change	☐	☐	☐	☐	☐
Experimentation was encouraged but monitored	☐	☐	☐	☐	☐
Corporate knowledge and experience was valued	☐	☐	☐	☐	☐
Provision was made for additional training and development to meet the needs of the change process	☐	☐	☐	☐	☐
The budget provided for the additional costs of transition	☐	☐	☐	☐	☐
New technology and capital and the induction of employees to them was included in the program	☐	☐	☐	☐	☐
Information and communication was of a high order	☐	☐	☐	☐	☐
People were listened to and received feedback at all stages	☐	☐	☐	☐	☐
Employees were involved in the design of the new workplace	☐	☐	☐	☐	☐
There were realistic scales of change within the scope of current and future resources	☐	☐	☐	☐	☐
Human and other resources were provided in addition to those required for maintaining day-to-day operations	☐	☐	☐	☐	☐

Trust, openness, honesty, transparency and involvement
were the keystones to change ☐ ☐ ☐ ☐ ☐

Strategies for implementation were clearly identified ☐ ☐ ☐ ☐ ☐

Time and space were allowed for progressive implementation ☐ ☐ ☐ ☐ ☐

Consultation with the employees responsible for change was
a high priority ☐ ☐ ☐ ☐ ☐

Careful consideration was given to the extent to which jobs,
work practices and team combinations were restructured ☐ ☐ ☐ ☐ ☐

Evaluation of the changes was and is on-going and involves
feedback to all concerned ☐ ☐ ☐ ☐ ☐

Consider the following scenario: You are the person responsible for the day-to-day supervision of Project X in a large-scale organisation. One of your most senior and experienced employees is promoted to a position in another organisation. You inform the General Manager that you will immediately set in motion the procedures for recruitment and will have the details on the table the next morning for consideration.

The next morning the human resources manager informs you the replacement will be the daughter of the General Manager, who has just completed her university degree. When you inform the human resources manager that the due procedures had not been followed in this appointment he says, 'You go and tell her, mate. She is the boss, you know.'

What are the implications of this appointment for the organisation?

_____

_____

_____

_____

What are the implications for you as supervisor?

_____

_____

_____

_____

What are the implications for the human resources manager?

_____

_____

_____

_____

What are the implications for the other employees?

_____

_____

_____

_____

What are the implications for the General Manager?

_____

_____

_____

_____

Do you intend to raise concern or lodge a complaint?

_____

_____

_____

_____

To whom will you present your case?

_____

_____

_____

_____

What would you have done first had you anticipated that the GM was likely to appoint her own daughter?

_____

_____

_____

_____

The cost of losing an experienced employee and the hiring of their replacement is estimated to be between $50 000 and $60 000.

Cost of staff turnover

Work out what would be the average cost to your organisation or section if this were to happen, taking the following budget as a guideline. (You may wish to add or delete items as applicable.)

	Cost $
Termination pay of leaving employee	_____
Loss of production or services (i.e. increased work hours of remaining employees)	_____
Extra administration costs incurred	_____
Advertising/agency fees	_____
Induction and training of new employee	_____
Other (specify)_____	_____
Total cost to company/section	$_____

Hiring the right person in the first place reduces these costs by reducing staff turnover. Finding the right person means making a commitment to anti-discriminatory practices in employee relations.

Do you perceive any link between the resignation rate and any discriminatory practices within your company?

_____

_____

_____

Is there a commitment from senior management and supervisors in support of the development of a supportive environment free from discrimination?

_____

_____

_____

Merit, diversity and equal employment opportunity

In order to fully analyse how effective your anti-discrimination practices are, answer the following questions:

What proportion of current employees were selected on genuine merit?

_____

_____

_____

What do you need to do to improve this area?

_____

_____

_____

To what extent does each employee have the opportunity to develop their potential?

_____

_____

_____

Does your training and development program provide for the needs of individual differences?

_____

_____

_____

How might this be improved?

_____

_____

_____

Has any attempt been made to link the diversity of the workforce with the diversity in the markets or suppliers?

_____

_____

_____

Has an equal employment opportunity policy been put in place?

_____

_____

_____

Are all employment procedures analysed, evaluated and reviewed on a regular basis?

_____

_____

_____

Consider the following scenarios and then for each one work out your answers to these questions in relation to how you would respond.

- Do you feel the employee was treated fairly?
- What are the implications for all the parties concerned?
- What could have been done to better manage the situation while it was occurring?
- What would be the implications if the outcome had been different?
- What steps would you recommend to resolve the matter or reduce the impact of the incident in the workplace?
- Outline the most appropriate steps that can be taken for each individual affected by the incident?
- What procedures and training will you need to put in place to raise awareness and prevent the incident from occurring again?

1. Political moves

Mary was employed by a food processing company. She was responsible for maintaining the smooth operation of the machine that puts lids on the cans. She was married to Roy, the supervisor of the warehouse. Last year one of their children died in a road accident and Mary suffered an emotional breakdown. Following this Mary and Roy's marriage fell apart and they were divorced.

Mary found it increasingly difficult to work with her former husband but she needed her job because she now had to be financially independent and had custody of her and Roy's two remaining teenage children. Mary often called in sick and sometimes had to leave work early due to emotional stress. Her condition was further aggravated by the general manager's constant criticism of her performance.

Roy was friendly with the general manager and he told him that Mary was 'hitting the bottle', which was why her work was poor and was endangering her section of the production line. The general manager informed Mary that he was dismissing her immediately, and that she would receive two weeks salary in lieu of notice.

2. Serious allegations

Gareth was a sales manager for a large hardware firm. He had a dynamic personality combined with a very friendly approach. He got on well with fellow employees and clients alike and most people found it difficult to say no to Gareth's persuasive and persistent approach and his ability to put fun into the formula. He was seen by many as someone who was always good for a joke and a laugh, even though many of his jokes were rude or crude. The calenders on his office wall, admittedly obtained from suppliers, were usually of nude women and he sometimes asked the female staff if they were like the girls in the photos. He developed a reputation as a 'ladies man' and it was often rumoured that he had affairs with some of the female staff. Because of Gareth's value to the organisation, management brushed aside these stories as mere rumours.

Gareth's secretary, Rebecca, comes to you and outlines her concerns about Gareth's behaviour. She tells you that on many occasions prior to this he would sit close to her at the desk and touch her, even to the point of massaging her neck, despite her protests. While she felt uncomfortable about this, she had not complained because she was new, young and desperate to keep her job. She had also felt compelled to laugh at his crude jokes and to join him and other staff members for drinks after work in order to be seen to be part of the team. She saw that other female employees seemed to enjoy Gareth's company; everyone appeared to like him so she tried to dismiss her uneasy feelings. But Gareth's behaviour got worse as time went by and he began to press her for kisses and cuddles.

At the office Christmas party she tried to avoid Gareth's attention, making excuses to go to the toilet, etc. But the stress of his overtures and the fact that he kept refilling her glass meant she drank too much. Gareth suggested she get some fresh air to walk off the effects of the drink. She said he kissed and cuddled her before lowering her to the ground. She said that she tried to resist but despite her protestations he undressed her and then had sex with her. She felt helpless and feared for her safety. She also felt embarrassed, wondering what the other staff would think of her. Now she is unsure of what to do.

3. Injury hazards

Charlie worked as a general hand and delivery person in the yard of a large building supplies company. Five years ago he injured his back when he fell from a stack of timber. To overcome his injury, the company trained him on how to lift heavy articles and purchased a fork lift to make his work more efficient and easier to handle. However, Charlie still did much of the work manually and this aggravated the injury. He could no longer do his job but because of his commitment, dedication and desire to continue working, Charlie was given the opportunity to work in the office. His duties included light work such as posting, filing, sorting, printing and light courier work. He didn't like the work or being in an office but persisted in order to support his family.

Elizabeth, one of the senior clerical staff, comes to you to say that all the administrative staff are frustrated with Charlie because they feel he is not very bright and constantly needs help, even with the simplest of tasks. They feel his poor performance reflects on the efficiency of their unit and he is creating extra work for them. The staff wants Charlie to be either sacked or moved to another department.

You raise the matter with the manager and he decides to give Charlie more training on how to better coordinate his work and work well with the others. He organises for health specialists to give Charlie therapy to ease the pain and teach him how to better manage his condition. The office staff, however, are still not happy and they continue to isolate Charlie. They make his life as uncomfortable as possible in the hope that he will resign or find another job. The manager explains to the staff that it is better to have Charlie working rather than going out on sick pay or worker's compensation. The staff say they understand this, but Charlie is not working out.

Charlie had always been a friendly, happy, cooperative, dedicated person who got on easily with everyone, so he found the attitude of the office staff extremely stressful, to the point that it was affecting his general health. This morning Charlie was sorting the mail and he suffered a massive heart attack. He died in the ambulance on the way to the hospital. He was 43 years old.

4. Representative dilemma

Martin is a machinist at a clothing company. He is caught stealing by his supervisor, who reports the incident to the general manager. The general manager dismisses Martin, ordering that the cost of the materials be deducted from his severance pay.

Martin demands support from the union. Betty, the union representative, wants to discuss the matter with the general manager, but he refuses to see her. He sends a message that this is a criminal matter and has nothing to do with the union. Betty talks to the regional union organiser who tells her the matter will need to be taken to the industrial commission as an unfair dismissal case.

Betty comes to you because she is concerned about the forthcoming hearing and the expectations demanded of her and her colleagues. She understands it is her duty to represent the rights of a union member at a hearing, regardless of what she thinks of the person. But she feels that Martin did steal the material and is therefore reluctant to speak on his behalf.

Colleen, who has been appointed the representative of the company at the hearing, also expresses to you her concerns about the case. She feels compromised in that she knows the general manager is spending company funds on weekends away with his secretary, claiming they are conference expenses, which is stealing as well. She also feels that she and Betty work well together, have respect for each other, and that this case may damage their good relationship.

5. Violent fallout

Judith works as the senior teller of a bank. Each afternoon she is responsible for ensuring all the customers leave and the door is locked. One day as she is about to close the door, two masked men with sawn-off shotguns burst in and one puts her in a headlock. He jams the gun up against her head. The other man fires a shot into the ceiling and demands that all the staff lie down or Judith will be shot.

The manager tries to resist and is struck with the butt of the gun, which breaks his arm. Judith is dragged behind the counter and ordered to fill the bags with cash. She stumbles and is slapped across the face and told to hurry. As the robbers leave they drag Judith with them and bundle her into a getaway car, leaving orders that she will be killed if anyone calls the police. Judith is blindfolded and driven to another location where the robbers get out. They warn her not to move, or else. After some time she gets out of the car and is found by a passerby and taken to the hospital.

Two weeks later she returns to work but increasingly finds it difficult. She is tense, cannot sleep, has frightening dreams, hallucinates and suffers anxiety and depression. She also has deep pangs of guilt because she believes that she was responsible for letting the robbers into the bank.

6. Loyalty to whom

The miners of a huge organisation are contracted as employees but are paid bonuses when their team exceeds the targetted output. It is therefore important for all the members of the team to work together to ensure they meet their targets. Colin's team of four has worked effectively together for almost eight years. Recently, however, one of the team members, Johnny, has not been putting in the same effort as his mates. This has affected the overall performance of the team and their bonuses have been reduced. The other members of the team are concerned. Colin has spoken to Johnny a number of times and has always been assured by Johnny that his work will improve. After a period where Johnny does a reasonable share of work, however, he slips back into his bad habits.

Colin notices that Johnny tends to stay in the pub long after the others go home. The day after these sessions Johnny is slow at work and tends to fall asleep on the job. Working in a mine means that Colin and his mates have a strong union background and under no circumstances will they inform management of Johnny's problem. They talk to Johnny about his excessive drinking but he abuses them and tells them to mind their own business.

Andrew, a well-respected engineer who has the responsibility for their area of operations, receives an anonymous phone call one day advising him to visit a certain tunnel in the mine. When Andrew arrives he finds Johnny asleep in a dark corner and immediately dismisses him because Johnny's actions are considered a serious breach of safety procedures. The union, supported by the other team members, represent Johnny at a hearing even though they know he is guilty of sleeping on the job and that it is a sackable offence.

To evaluate how well your organisation meets the requirements of the occupational health and safety legislation, work through the following questions.

The policy
Does your company have an occupational health and safety policy?

When was it formulated?

Who was involved in its formulation?

Does it require revision?

To what extent are employees given the opportunity to contribute to the ongoing revision of the policy and its guidelines?

Is there an occupational health and safety committee?

Who is represented on that committee?

Does this representation cover all sections of the organisation?

_____

_____

_____

_____

_____

_____

Communicating the policy
Does every employee have a copy of the policy?

Is it included in the induction manual for all new employees?

Is it incorporated into operational procedural documents?

Are the policies, guidelines and signs in the office written in plain English and, where necessary, other languages?

Are emergency procedures displayed where all staff can read them, particularly at every exit?

_____

_____

_____

_____

_____

_____

Training and knowledge

Have all supervisors and managers attended a training program on occupational health and safety?

Have all staff been trained in occupational health and safety?

Are there emergency procedures in place?

_____

_____

_____

_____

_____

Equipment safety

What procedures are in place to ensure the safety of equipment and machinery?

How do you ensure the safety of the building or site?

Is the office layout, furniture and equipment ergonomically suitable to prevent injury or aggravation?

Is there sufficient safety equipment for the handling of hazardous materials?

What fire equipment is on hand?

How often is it checked?

_____

_____

_____

_____

_____

Responsibility

Is risk management a key performance responsibility of every supervisor and manager?

Is there a key person responsible for risk management and emergency procedures?

To whom can employees go with concerns about safety and health?

Which personnel have been trained for the safe handling of equipment and hazardous materials?

Who is responsible for the fire equipment?

Are there fire wardens to manage emergencies?

_____

_____

_____

_____

_____

activity 10 — Types of employment

The world of work is changing at an ever increasing rate. Not only are people changing their jobs on average about every three to four years, but they are being employed under different conditions. The number of full-time positions is decreasing but the number of part-time positions is increasing at a greater figure. More and more functions are also being outsourced to contract workers who operate as independent sole traders. The other big increase is in the employment of temporary employees at an hourly rate. These 'employees' do not require the on-costs of superannuation and leave entitlements of permanent employees. Many operate from home.

Look first at your own organisation

What are the advantages of using contract or hired temporary staff?

What are the disadvantages of using these forms of employment?

In which areas of your organisation could temporary staff be best utilised?

Are there any functions that could be contracted out to independent operators?

What would be the reaction of current permanent employees to a change in the number of temporary and contract workers?

_____

_____

_____

_____

_____

_____

_____

_____

_____

Look now to your own personal situation

If you were made redundant today would you consider operating as a temporary employee through a hire agency?

Would you consider setting up as a private contractor?

What would be the advantages and disadvantages?

As a private contractor, what would you have to do to compensate for the loss of benefits you had as a permanent employee?

Are you the type of person who can cope easily with change, is flexible, can think and act quickly, is not afraid to make decisions and are prepared to work in situations where there are far fewer promotional opportunities?

Would you be willing to work outside regular hours—at night and at weekends—to get a contract?

How would you calculate your worth in contracting terms?

Could you command a fee that more than meets your current salary package plus the additional expenses of taxation, private superannuation and insurance, office, equipment, transport, supplies, advertising, marketing, holidays, etc., etc.?

_____

_____

_____

_____

_____

_____

_____

_____

_____

activity **11** *Training and development*

In many organisations the emphasis of training and development programs is on the acquisition of technical skills and the use of new equipment and technology. Other needs, such as the preparation for new taxation requirements and accounting procedures, have a high priority. But people are the most important resource in any organisation and therefore matters relating to the people business should have the highest priority. Which of the following areas are included in your training, development and induction programs?

- Dealing with conflict
- Negotiation, mediation and conciliation skills
- Recruitment and selection procedures
- Equal employment opportunity and anti-discrimination
- Occupational health and safety
- Risk management
- Effective communication skills
- Career-path planning
- Team building
- Customer service
- First aid
- Enterprise bargaining
- Supervision and leadership skills
- Employee relations
- Job analysis and design
- Performance appraisal, management and development
- Interview skills
- Reporting on performance
- Human resource information systems
- Human resource planning
- Change management

List each of the above in some order of priority for your organisation.

_____

_____

_____

Determine who would gain the most from each of these programs.

_____
_____
_____

Is it necessary to bring in outside experts to conduct these programs?

_____
_____
_____

Is it appropriate and affordable for some people to attend outside courses?

_____
_____
_____

What programs can be conducted internally with the whole team present?

_____
_____
_____

What are the benefits of in-house programs?

_____
_____
_____

What are the benefits of taking people out of the work environment for training?

_____
_____
_____

How is the training budget proportioned between management and workers?

_____
_____
_____

Suggest major changes to your training and development program.

_____
_____
_____

activity 12 — Consultation

Assess the extent to which your organisation is committed to genuine consultation with its employees by rating the following approaches in terms of importance in your section or organisation. Rate from 1 to 5, with 5 being the highest.

Consultation approach	1	2	3	4	5
Make the decision and then tell them about it.	☐	☐	☐	☐	☐
Make the decision and then sell the idea by sharing the information.	☐	☐	☐	☐	☐
Make the decision and then make minor modifications after listening to their responses.	☐	☐	☐	☐	☐
Propose a plan, provide the information, listen, ask and then decide.	☐	☐	☐	☐	☐
Ask for ideas, listen to the responses and then decide.	☐	☐	☐	☐	☐
Set up a consultative committee to consider alternatives.	☐	☐	☐	☐	☐
Set up a consultative committee to negotiate an appropriate outcome.	☐	☐	☐	☐	☐

Do the employees want to have a say in decision making?

_____

_____

_____

_____

Are the managers willing to listen to the ideas of the employees?

_____

_____

_____

_____

Is there a willingness to share information?

_____

_____

_____

_____

Is there a culture of joint problem solving?

_____
_____
_____
_____

Is the management willing to commit time and budget to a consultative committee?

_____
_____
_____
_____

Is there agreement in principle between the management and employees that a joint problem-solving approach through a consultative committee is the best way to go?

_____
_____
_____
_____

How might consultative processes be improved in your organisation?

_____
_____
_____
_____

Consider each of the following matters and determine the extent to which they could be an avenue for consultation and negotiation in the decision-making process. Write N/A against the item if you believe that it is not appropriate for employees to be involved in the discussion or negotiation leading to decision making. Against the others place a number 1 to 5, with 5 being the highest, indicating its relative importance to the involvement of employees.

Matters for consultation and negotiation	1	2	3	4	5
Health, safety and welfare	☐	☐	☐	☐	☐
The layout of the physical working environment	☐	☐	☐	☐	☐
Skills audit	☐	☐	☐	☐	☐
Skills acquisition	☐	☐	☐	☐	☐
Jobs classification and redesign	☐	☐	☐	☐	☐
Improving customer service	☐	☐	☐	☐	☐
Improving effectiveness and productivity	☐	☐	☐	☐	☐
Evaluating competitor's products and services	☐	☐	☐	☐	☐
Setting targets	☐	☐	☐	☐	☐
Developing effective procedural manuals	☐	☐	☐	☐	☐
Performance appraisal and management	☐	☐	☐	☐	☐
Training and development	☐	☐	☐	☐	☐
Continuous improvement	☐	☐	☐	☐	☐
Recruitment	☐	☐	☐	☐	☐
Selection	☐	☐	☐	☐	☐
Equal employment opportunity	☐	☐	☐	☐	☐
Recognition and reward	☐	☐	☐	☐	☐
Career-path planning	☐	☐	☐	☐	☐
Communication strategies	☐	☐	☐	☐	☐
Marketing	☐	☐	☐	☐	☐
Flexibility and hours of duty	☐	☐	☐	☐	☐
Rosters	☐	☐	☐	☐	☐
Leave provisions	☐	☐	☐	☐	☐
Implementation of new technology	☐	☐	☐	☐	☐

Restructuring	☐	☐	☐	☐	☐
Enterprise bargaining	☐	☐	☐	☐	☐
Child care	☐	☐	☐	☐	☐

In which areas would you extend the level of employee consultation and negotiation in your organisation?

_____

_____

_____

_____

You have been selected to represent the employer in negotiations leading to the signing of a new enterprise agreement. The general manager informs you that the future viability of the enterprise depends on keeping costs to a minimum, especially in the area of labour. He indicates that he does not want labour costs to increase by more than 2 per cent per annum and any increases should be offset by increases in productivity.

How will you prepare your case?

_____

_____

What research and information will be necessary?

_____

_____

Who will you involve in your team?

_____

_____

What will be the key factors in your proposal?

_____

_____

What reaction do you anticipate from the employees and their union?

_____

_____

How will you address their expected concerns?

_____

_____

What do you expect to be their counter proposal?

_____

_____

How will you address their anticipated proposal?

_____

_____

How do you see productivity improving without sacrificing the legal requirements that protect workers' rights?

_____

_____

How will these affect the costs to the organisation on one side and the work arrangements for the employees on the other?

_____

_____

What are you willing to exchange for increased input and productivity gains by the workers?

_____

_____

What do you expect the workers could exchange for increased benefits?

_____

_____

At what point do you anticipate the final agreement will be reached?

_____

_____

What will be the major hurdles that have to be overcome to reach that agreement?

_____

_____

How do you propose to overcome those hurdles?

_____

_____

What time span are you allowing to complete the agreement?

_____

_____

How will you convince your general manager that his proposals are unreasonable in the light of the current environment?

_____

_____

How will you ensure that the agreement, when signed, will be implemented as per the terms agreed upon?

_____

_____

activity 15 — *What now for the future?*

If you are serious about improving the working environment and the relationships between employees and management you need to take time out now to reflect on what you have done in the past, assess how effective you have been and then propose changes to improve those matters in the future. To do this, use the following questions to compile your assessment.

Which employee relations strategies have been the most effective in the past?

_____

_____

_____

Which of these have worked so well that you will continue to use them in the future?

_____

_____

_____

Which have been useful without being outstanding and therefore will require some modification in the future?

_____

_____

_____

Which strategies will you stop using because they are not achieving the desired outcomes?

_____

_____

_____

What practices must be stopped because they are negative, destructive or against current legislation?

_____

_____

_____

What practices must be stopped because they are not in harmony with company policy and culture?

_____

_____

_____

What new strategies will be tried in order to improve the health, safety and security of the working environment?

_____

_____

_____

How can we improve the working relationships with employees, supervisors and managers?

_____

_____

_____

How can we improve the manner by which we consult and negotiate issues as an on-going process?

_____

_____

_____

In general terms, what type of a working organisation are we trying to develop?

_____

_____

_____